GOD IS NOT A REPUBLICAN

GOD
IS NOT A
REPUBLICAN

BENJAMIN P. DIXON

PUBLISHED BY

JACKSONVILLE, FLORIDA

God is Not a Republican
Copyright ©2012 Benjamin P. Dixon

Edited By Tamera Stanford Purnell
Contributing Editor: P. Scott Dixon

PUBLISHED BY EAST & 42ND PUBLISHING, JACKSONVILLE, FLORIDA

ISBN-13: 978-0-9835566-2-6 ISBN-10: 0-9835566-2-8
First Edition

All Scripture quotations, unless otherwise indicated, are taken from the King James Version. Scripture quotations marked (NKJV) are taken from the New King James Version® copyright ©1982 by Thomas Nelson Inc. Used by permission. All rights reserved. Scripture quotations marked (ESV) are taken from The Holy Bible, English Standard Version, copyright © 2001 by Crossway Bibles, a division of Good News Publishers. Used by permission. All rights reserved. Scripture quotations marked (NIV) are taken from the Holy Bible, New International Version®. NIV®. Copyright © 1973, 1978, 1984 by International Bible Society. Used by permission of Zondervan Publishing House. All Rights Reserved. Scripture quotations marked (AMP) are taken from the Amplified Bible®. Copyright© 1954, 1958, 1962, 1964, 1965, 1987 by The Lockman Foundation. Used by permission of Zondervan Publishing House. Scripture quotations marked (NLT) are taken from the Holy Bible, New Living Translation, copyright © 1996, 2004, 2007 by Tyndale House Foundation. Used by permission of Tyndale House Publishers, Inc., Carol Stream, Illinois 60188. All rights reserved.

All rights reserved. No part of this publication may be reproduced or transmit-ted in any form or by any means, electronic or mechanical, including photocopying, recording, or any other information storage and retrieval system without the written permission of the publisher, except in the case of brief quotations embodied in critical articles or reviews.

Cover Design by Adrian Gray and Benjamin Dixon

Printed in the United States of America
10 9 8 7 6 5 4 3 2

For Dada

Rev. Dr. Percy M. Dixon
(1944-2005)

You would have been my primary source for this book. How I would have loved to talk to you all night long about these issues. Thankfully, you left a portion of your gift in each of us. I hope we make you proud.

CONTENTS

Introduction ix

Prologue 15

Chapter 1: Oppressive Freedom 25

Section 1: God's Politics and the Issues 35

Chapter 2: God's Politics: How Would Jesus Vote? 37

Chapter 3: Missed Opportunities: Abortion Debate 51

Chapter 4: Gay Rights and Marriage Equality 67

Chapter 5: Healthcare 77

Chapter 6: Black and White: Equally Conservative, Equally Divided 89

Section 2: Economic Morality 103

    About this Section 104

Chapter 7: The God of Justice 107

Chapter 8: Kingdom of God Economics 115

Chapter 9: Morality of Capitalism and the Free Markets 123

Chapter 10: The Moral Imperatives of Taxation 137

CONTENTS

Chapter 11: Secular Case for Economic Morality   147

Section 3: Conservatism   155

Chapter 12: The Conservative Religion   157

Chapter 13: Conservative Contradictions   169

Section 4: The Role of Christianity in America   175

Chapter 14: The Faith of a President   177

Chapter 15: Faith of our Fathers   187

Chapter 16: True Christianity in Politics   195

Afterword   203

Notes   211

Bibliography   225

Index   241

INTRODUCTION

It is likely that the Republican Party would not exist today if not for the Christian Evangelical vote.[1] The mobilization of the Christian voting bloc revolutionized the political landscape that otherwise may have been dominated by the Democratic Party.[2] This political coalition is so complete that today, Evangelical Christianity is nearly synonymous with Republican.

Hundreds of thousands of Christian voters wrestle within themselves because of their deep spiritual convictions, their political beliefs, and the notion that in order to be a serious Christian you must vote Republican.

Much of modern Christianity has strayed away from its true meaning: followers of Christ.[3] Christianity, by most beliefs, is an internal work of becoming more like Jesus. Emphasis may vary by denomination, but one thing remains the same: being like Christ requires us to examine ourselves and to change those things about us that are not like Him. Being Christian is about seeking forgiveness and forgiving. It is a personal affair.

Unfortunately, many have transformed Christianity into a bludgeoning tool that self-righteously allows us to believe that others need to change into being more like us. Although very few Christians will ever put it so bluntly, the reality is that our faith has become less about changing our personal behavior and character and more about telling others what they need to change. Christ never forced himself on anyone. He never condemned those who were not like Him. He simply presented them with a choice then gave them the freedom to make up their own minds.

People of faith often look to politicians to enact legislation which would make America more "Christian." All that was ever needed for our nation to be more Christian was Christians who acted more like Christ and demonstrated His love to the world; however, instead of the world knowing us by the love that we demonstrate or by the example we have set with our personal lives, too often, they have known us by our zealotry.

Christians have been preoccupied with bringing prayer back to schools, ending abortions, opposing gay rights, and other political issues that we have been told should define our political participation as Christians.

As we will discuss throughout this book, none of these issues can be achieved without infringing on the rights of segments of citizens in America where the founding principle is freedom. Therefore, much of what we have been told should be the focal point of Christian political participation is virtually unattainable because it violates the freedoms that the Constitution guarantees.

This book is not an attack on the Republican Party. Clearly God is neither Republican nor Democrat, but few would ever try to assert that God was the latter. Furthermore, this is not an attack on the pastors that inadvertently delivered us into the hands of an amoral political party. Many of them were simply trying to further the cause of Christ. However, this book is an unabashed attack on the pervasive manipulation of the faithful that has taken place for more than thirty years. This book is aimed at helping Christians understand that God is bigger than any single-issue, political party or interest group.

My hope is that those Christians who have struggled back and forth between their faith and their politics would come to the realization that we are free to vote for whichever candidate we feel best represents us. My sincerest prayer is that as you read this book your eyes will be opened to the different ways in

Introduction

which many sincere Christians have been compelled by pastors and manipulated by politicians for an entire generation.

To the nonbelievers, adherents of other religions, agnostics, and atheists who are reading this book, what follows is a conversation between Christians. Although we may not agree on the underlying premise that God exists, and that Jesus is Lord, we can agree that Christianity—like many other religions that fall prey to the ambitions of men—has been manipulated long enough. I hope that you would not read this book with antipathy towards religion but, rather, with the understanding that this is a Christian dilemma that can only be resolved by using what we believe to be biblical truths and what we all agree to be constitutional truths. Moreover, I believe we desire the same result: to see the end of both the manipulation of religion for political gain and the gross misrepresentation of what Jesus stood for.

...It is apparently necessary for me to state once again—not what kind of church I believe in, for that should be important only to me—but what kind of America I believe in. I believe in an America where the separation of church and state is absolute—where no Catholic prelate would tell the President (should he be Catholic) how to act, and no Protestant minister would tell his parishioners for whom to vote.

John F. Kennedy

September 12, 1960

Prologue

HOUSTON: 1980[4]

The stage was set.[5] Across the platform sat the most influential Christian pastors of the day including Jerry Falwell, James Robison, and James Kennedy. In the audience sat thousands of other pastors, representing nearly 50 million parishioners.[6] They all gathered at the nonpartisan *National Affairs Briefing*, which had been billed as one of the most important gatherings in the history of Christian Evangelicals. At the time, this billing may have been hyperbole. Indeed, history would prove it prophetic.

James Robison, the young, idealistic pastor from Houston, was both the visionary and the brains behind the event. Robison was known for his brash sermons and rhetoric. That day was no different. He took to the stage and spoke words that would echo for a generation:

> The perverts and the liberals and the leftists and the communists [are all] coming out of the closets. It is time for God's people to come out of the closet, out of the churches, and change America![7]

Whether one agreed with Robison's words or considered them to be hate speech, there was no denying the power and authority with which he spoke them. Whether good or bad, his sermon sent chills down the spines of all who listened in the audience that day and those who would hear it in the years to come. Perhaps the only thing more powerful than Robison's words was the presence of the one with whom he and the other evangelical pastors shared the stage: presidential candidate, Ronald Reagan.

Reagan did not fit the profile of a politician that would be campaigning at a religious event. His background had not been a particularly religious one. He was known more for his days in Hollywood as an actor than he was for being a man of faith.[8] His campaign staff was reluctant about him even participating in Robison's event. To their horror, Reagan did not wait until it was his time to speak to enter the stage.[9] Being the consummate public figure that he was, it is likely that he understood the value of a church audience watching him listen to the preacher speaking rather than only saying a few words and leaving before the sermon.[10]

There Reagan sat as the lone candidate, sharing the stage with the same Evangelical pastors that only four years prior helped elect his rival, Jimmy Carter. These pastors represented a tremendous number of potential voters, and so it is unlikely that the other candidates were not aware of the political value of attending the event. For years, this audience had been carefully and meticulously groomed to become the most powerful voting bloc in the Republican Party.

Great irony lies in the fact that Ronald Reagan shared the stage that day in 1980 instead of Jimmy Carter. In 1976, nearly fifty percent of Evangelicals voted for Carter.[11] He was considered, by many, to be the first Evangelical president in the history of the United States. He was by far the most openly reverent. While the rest of the Washington Establishment tuned into *Meet the Press* for their Sunday morning edification, President Carter turned to his local congregation to seek God and to offer worship. Carter not only attended his local congregation during his presidency, he privately taught Sunday School whenever the opportunity presented itself.[12]

Presidents have always sought the counsel of the great spiritual leaders of their day; however, these moments were often the byproduct of dilemmas and difficult times, personal indiscretions, or political calculation. For Jimmy Carter, faith was something too personal and sacred to dilute with politics. He had a personal relationship with Christ; one in which he boldly sought God of his own accord without the need of a political pastor. His actions were looked upon as strange and foreign by beltway insiders; yet, those same actions were affirmations of faith to millions of Christians across the nation.[13] For the first time in many decades, Evangelical Christianity had returned to the mainstream and to the forefront of the nation.[14]

THE STAGE WAS SET

The stage was set. If any politician's faith and personal witness could earn him the right to be seated next to the nation's leading Evangelical pastors, the seat surely would have belonged to Jimmy Carter. Yet, President Carter was not present. The seat, which was his four years earlier, was filled instead by the former Hollywood star and political rival, Ronald Reagan. This was despite the fact that Reagan was not a conservative evangelical even by the church's definition.[15]

Nevertheless, something happened between 1976 and 1980; something that changed the face of the American political landscape for a generation. A man whose faith in Christ that was so bold that it confused the Washington Establishment now found himself an outcast from his own brethren. Like Joseph, he was the target of his brothers' anger.[16] Carter had been invited to attend the National Affairs Briefing; however, he was wise enough to know that the seat, which was once his because of his sincere faith, was now Reagan's because of his politics.[17]

1976-1980: TURNING OF THE TIDE

American culture was changing in a dramatic fashion during the sixties and Seventies. *Roe v. Wade* legalized abortions.[18] Prayer in schools had been deemed unconstitutional.[19] Homosexuality was coming into the mainstream. The height of racial tensions in our nation was less than a decade in the past. America was changing.

Pastors across the nation began to fear that the moral fabric of American society had been completely eroded. Fiery sermons of preachers taking a stand against the moral decay of a once great moral society were preached across the pulpits and airwaves of America.

Many of these preachers felt that America needed a spiritual revival. Others thought that a spiritual revolution needed to take place. Some held to the traditional view of Christianity, believing that the moral renewal would take place in the heart of the individual. Others believed that this spiritual revolution was to be an actual revolution which needed to take place on the national level through politics. One thing the pastors of this era agreed, something needed to be done to save the soul of America.[20]

The Republican Attraction

1976 was deemed "The Year of the Evangelical."[21] Millions of Christians were affiliated with televangelists who broadcasted on weekly and daily basis into homes across the nation. The same pastors who were seated on stage with Ronald Reagan that day in Houston had, for many years, wielded tremendous influence over a growing number of Americans. Each of these television pastors represented a national network of Christians organized into mailing lists that rivaled that of either political party. These lists were considered extremely valuable and held tightly by the television ministries. While access to these mailing lists was limited, knowledge of their existence was wide spread.[22] While some pastors sought to inspire this spiritual renewal on the individual level, others looked to convert their religious influence into political capital. Whatever the reasons, these televangelists plunged themselves into the political realm, bringing along with them their entire congregations and both the name and reputation of Christ.

Prologue

History Repeats Itself

This was not the first time influential pastors had been targeted by political parties. Throughout our nation's history, presidents and other leaders have sought the counsel of great preachers. From Harry Truman to George W. Bush, Billy Graham's ministry impacted the halls of the White House to the highest degree. Graham's relationship with Richard Nixon was the most noteworthy. During the Nixon Administration, Graham was recruited to facilitate Sunday worship services at the White House. This was a first in American history.

Charles Colson, Special Counsel to President Nixon, was responsible for arranging the Sunday services. He commented on the relationship between pastors and the White House:

> [Pastors] would be dazzled by the aura of the Oval Office, and I found them to be about the most pliable of any of the special interest groups that we worked with.[23]

While Colson arranged the White House Sunday services, Billy Graham delivered the weekly sermon. Colson's responsibility was to ensure that all the necessary political figures and Christian businessmen were invited to attend. Upon reflection on his duties, he admitted that there were occasions in which Nixon was sincere in his pursuit of God. However, he was certain that, at all times, the services were calibrated for the maximum political gain.[25] Later in life, he noted:

> One of the reasons I have written books and given speeches warning Christian leaders not to be seduced by the wiles and the attractiveness of power in the White House, and to keep our distance and never mix the gospel with politics, is that I saw how well I exploited religious leaders when I was in that job. But that's what politicians do.[24]

GOD IS NOT A REPUBLICAN

THE MORAL MAJORITY

While some influential pastors looked to exert their influence in the political world, Republican strategists looked for pastors whom they could bring into the Party.[26] Republican strategist, Morton Blackwell, knew that, at that time, conservatives stood little chance of electing a candidate without widening their political base; they needed to recruit millions of new Republicans. Blackwell regarded Evangelical Christians as "the greatest tract of virgin timber on the political landscape."[27] Upon this realization, Morton, along with several other strategists, began to target influential pastors whom they could mold and who, in turn, would be willing to deliver their congregations to the Republican Party.[28]

In 1979 Jerry Falwell, the de facto leader of the evangelical movement, was approached by four Republican operatives at a meeting arranged by his associate, Robert Billings. They were: Paul Weyrich, Ed McAteer, Richard Viguerie, and Howard Phillips.[29] Each of these men had been longtime party activists. Each had social issues, which drove their political passions. Each was fully aware of the potential of the Evangelical vote.

Before this pivotal meeting, the Republican Party had minimal access to the burgeoning ministries and virtually no access to their extensive mailing lists. The Party needed a way to gain access to the invaluable religious network. At the same time, Jerry Falwell wanted to increase his political influence in order to further, what he believed to be, the will of God.[30] At the meeting, both sides found the very opportunity they had sought.

At this meeting, Paul Weyrich inadvertently spoke a phrase that Pastor Falwell felt was divinely inspired. It was the name for a movement the men surrounding the table believed would transform the nation: the Moral Majority.[31] Falwell seized the name, almost as an embrace of what he believed to be providence. In that moment, the Moral Majority was born, conceived

Prologue

by four Republican strategists looking to bring their particular interpretation of morality to the nation. In regards to the purpose of the Moral Majority, Falwell stated:

> We have a threefold primary responsibility. Number one: get people saved. Number two: get them baptized. Number three: get them registered to vote.[32]

Disillusioned with the liberal politics of their fellow evangelical, Jimmy Carter, conservative pastors were mobilized into political action with the express intention of voting Carter out of office. Colonel Doner, founder of the Christian Voice, stated in an interview:

> Christians gave Jimmy Carter his razor-thin margin of victory in 1976. We plan to reverse that in 1980.[33]

Fifty-five percent of evangelicals were registered to vote at the time the Moral Majority was founded—compared to the national average of seventy-two percent.[34] This low percentage was the result of many Christians believing, at the time, religion and politics should not be mixed. Voter registration became a primary focus of religiously conservative organizations. In two years, these organizations registered over two-million new Christian voters. Over eight million voters were registered in five years. Doner's words would prove prophetic.[35]

On display that day in Houston, 1980, was a shift in the political landscape that had been developing over many years. The Republican Party saw an opportunity to fill a void in their political platform with the energy and enthusiasm of social issue voters. For years, Conservative operatives in the party had been working on this strategy of carefully courting socially conservative pastors across the nation while hoping to recruit enough new voters to be elected into power.

All We Like Sheep?[36]

The heart of every sincere Christian is centered on Christ, His Kingdom, and the internal pursuit to be more like Him. The thing we want most as believers is to be pleasing to Christ. This pursuit often leaves us in a vulnerable position that too often is taken advantage of by ambitious preachers. The pastor-parishioner relationship is most often referred to as shepherd-sheep. This analogy is apt: wherever the shepherd leads, the sheep will follow; whether it is into a place of safety or into the mouths of wolves.

A generation ago, on a platform with the shepherds of millions of sheep, Ronald Reagan took his seat on stage and listened as James Robison rebuked Christians for being too passive in their politics. Falwell, Robertson, and so many other powerful pastors listened as James Robison prepared the way for Reagan. There, Reagan sat both confidently and comfortably as Robison compared liberals—and by extension the Democratic Party—to "perverts" and communists. The future president did not flinch as the audience celebrated with thunderous applause and cheers.[37]

Whether intentional or providential, the years of work by influential pastors and Republican strategists led to this moment. This moment had been meticulously prepared. The faithful sought a political leader who could reclaim the nation for moral values. The Republican Party had desperately looked for new voters who could help them reclaim political power.

Reagan was the linchpin. This moment in political history was uniquely ideal for his political capabilities. Reagan only needed to connect the two groups with his words; as fate would have it, communication was his greatest skill. To his awaiting audience, Reagan spoke words that would change a generation:

Prologue

I know this is a nonpartisan gathering; and so I know that you can't endorse me. I want you to know that I endorse you...[38]

With that, a handful of ideological—if not naïve—pastors delivered millions of faithful Christians into the hands of an amoral political party in hopes that the party would achieve great victories in the fight to restore traditional family values. As time would prove, the Republican Party achieved many victories; however, few were for the cause of morality.

1.

OPPRESSIVE FREEDOM

> There was a man who had two sons. The younger one said to his father, 'Father, give me my share of the estate.' So he divided his property between them. Not long after that, the younger...set off for a distant country and there squandered his wealth in wild living.
>
> After he had spent everything...he began to be in need. So he...hired himself out to a citizen of that country, who sent him to his fields to feed pigs. He longed to fill his stomach with the pods that the pigs were eating...
>
> When he came to his senses he said, 'How many of my father's hired servants have food to spare, and here I am starving to death! I will...go back to my father and say to him: Father...I am no longer worthy to be called your son; make me like one of your hired servants.' So he got up and went to his father." Luke 15:11-20 (NIV)[39]

If there is a single thread which connects each chapter in this book, it is the concept of *Oppressive Freedom*. This oxymoronic term came to me as I began to grapple with the nuances of what it meant to be free. In our youth, we tend to believe that freedom is the ability to do whatever we want whenever we want. Although many of us would never have used the word "oppressive" to describe the discipline our parents attempted to instill into us, we believed their actions were, at a minimum, restrictive.

Although we did not realize it at the time, it was the very discipline we hated that actually made us free. Discipline helps to maintain freedom. Our parents and guardians understood from experience what they were attempting to teach us through chores, lessons, and even biblical stories: unrestrained freedom can become oppressive.

The parable of the Prodigal Son is perhaps the best illustration of an "oppressive" type of freedom. The father honored the younger son's request to receive his inheritance earlier than he customarily would have. The younger son immediately left home and proceeded to do what most people who are unaccustomed to handling freedom do: they lose everything. The son did not have the wisdom or maturity to handle the freedom that he had away from his father's house.

The Prodigal Son was free to do whatever he wanted, whenever he wanted. No one was able to tell him what was right or wrong. There was no one to correct his missteps. He was so free that his freedom ultimately became oppressive. It was only after his experience of hitting rock-bottom that the son "came to himself" and determined to return to the structure that came with living in his father's house.

His father's house represented structure, rules and regulations, and law and order. The son did not physically need to be at his father's house for him to benefit from this structure and discipline. He merely needed to carry those lessons with him wherever he went. Yet, because he had left the safety of his father's home before he was mature enough to manage his freedom properly, he ended up living in the filth of swine, desperate enough to eat the swill the pigs ate.

This biblical lesson is synonymous with our liberties not only as Christians, but also as citizens of the United States. We are free as individuals to live our lives how we see fit. The father in the parable did not force his morals and beliefs on his son; similarly, neither does God. And if God does not force himself on us, then neither should any religion, political interest group, or the United States government. In fact, that is what the Constitution guarantees us: a government that cannot force us to live by another group's religious beliefs or moral code.

OPPRESSIVE FREEDOM IN AMERICA

As Americans, we have the right to squander all of our belongings to the point that we become destitute. We also have the right to be alcoholics, sex-addicts, and compulsive gamblers. There is no one to force us to eat healthy foods; therefore, we have the freedom to eat ourselves into high-blood pressure, diabetes, and heart-attacks. Likewise, we have the right to waste our time in school, to drop out, and to make as little of our lives as we choose. We also have the freedom to maximize every opportunity we are afforded in life. We are free to fight to become the best success we can be. The choice is ours.

Our freedoms are only limited in regards to how our actions affect other people or society as a whole. We are not free to infringe upon someone else's rights and freedoms. We are not free to cause others to live in fear. We are not free to force our religious beliefs on those who do not willingly accept them. Outside of these types of limitations, the government has no authority to regulate or limit our personal beliefs, morality, or decisions. We are free. So free, that if we wish, we can lead lives that will become oppressive. This is oppressive freedom.

There is no question that we could live healthier and longer lives if the government forced healthy eating standards on society. Likewise, no one would ever have to suffer through addictions if the government could somehow control all illicit substances and habits. Thousands of families would still be intact if entire incomes had not lost because the government outlawed gambling. Clearly, our lives could be better if we had never been exposed to all of the things that become oppressive.

However, as long as the government hides us from these things, we will never mature enough to handle them properly for ourselves. Furthermore, no reasonable citizen would want a government so powerful that it has the ability to dictate morality in the most minor details of our lives.

"Benevolent Father" or "Big Brother"

One of the most revealing differences between conservative and liberal thought is the role that both groups want the government to play in our personal lives. No matter what either political side says about "individual freedoms" or "limited roles government," both, on various issues, advocate for government infringement into our personal lives.

Ideology	Wants the Government Involved With	Does Not Want the Government Involved With
Conservative	Restricting Women's Right to Obtain Abortions	Charity, Poverty Relief, Maintaining Safety Net
	Defining and Defending Traditional Marriage	Using Tax Policy to Reduce Income Inequality
	Creating Business and Investment Incentives	Business or Environmental Regulations
	Buffeting "Moral Decay"	Ensuring Access to Healthcare
	Projecting American Power	Individual Health & Nutrition
Liberal	Reducing Income Inequality	A Woman's Reproductive Rights
	Ensuring Equality Under the Law Regardless of Age, Sex, Race or Sexual Orientation	Imposing Morality at the Expense of Individual Freedom
	Ensuring Equal Access to Healthcare	Empire Building
	Environmental Protection	World Policing
*This chart is a snapshot of today's political environment, as these standards change over time.		

The chart on the previous page is not an exhaustive list of conservative and liberal viewpoints. It is not meant to represent adherents of these ideologies as monolithic. It is simply meant to demonstrate the point that both sides seek government intervention and involvement on various issues that they have determined to be beneficial to the nation. The truest difference between conservative and liberal ideologies is best revealed by the reasons for which they seek the government to "father" us and to "protect" us from things that may harm us. On the opposite side of the coin, there are political issues that both ideologies want the government to stay out of. The latter demonstrates how both parties are like the Prodigal Son, seeking the opportunity to find their own way and to live life on their own terms. The former demonstrates how both parties are like the Prodigal Son's older brother—who stayed home seeking the father's knowledge, insight, and protection.

THE WISDOM OF THE FATHER

The prodigal father knew what was out there waiting for his son. He also knew the value of being able to make one's own decisions in life. He did not force the younger son to stay, nor did he force the older son to leave. He allowed them to make their own choices. The father in the parable knew what most parents know. We cannot hide our children from the realities of the world any more than our parents were able to hide us.

Nevertheless, it is the internal maturity and discipline that we learned along the way that truly allows us to be free. The Bible clearly outlines behaviors that are beneficial both to us as individuals and society as a whole; however, the Bible also makes it clear that God wants us to abide by those behaviors willingly: through free will.[40] Likewise, the Constitution simply created a method for us to live out our lives as freely as possible: by our own free will.

A Divinely Inspired Constitution?

If there is one biblical theme that is buried within the U.S. Constitution, it is our right as individuals to have freedom even if that freedom is so free that it becomes oppressive. We have the right to live our lives as we see fit. If the lifestyle that we choose becomes oppressive, then so be it. Although the Constitution does not outline behaviors for living our life in the manner as the Bible, it grants us the freedom to discover whatever moral compass we desire to be the guide our lives. In the same manner that the Prodigal Father granted his son moral freedom, the Constitution grants us the freedom to determine what moral code to live by, if any. Whatever we choose will ultimately determine our individual degree of freedom.

Because the core of the Constitution is the protection of free will, the Constitution has the power to prevent the conflicts that are inevitable when men attempt to dominate, regulate, or legislate the morality of other men. It is, perhaps, the only man made document capable of doing this. It protects us by mandating that we respect every individual's right to life, liberty, and their freedom to choose the code of conduct and morality to live by, so long as that conduct does not infringe upon another's freedom.

In many ways, the Constitution is the ultimate human protector of God's intent: to give individuals the freedom to define their existence for themselves. It is the most powerful non-religious and divinely inspired document in the history of this world. And yet, it is but a glimpse into one of the intents of our Creator's desire for our human experience on this earth: to mature on our own terms to the point that we can handle the tremendous responsibility of freedom and free will.

Oppressive Freedom

AMERICA'S OPPRESSIVE FREEDOM

Our struggles with individual freedom and having enough maturity to avoid its pitfalls are a microcosm of the struggle that the United States faces politically: the problem is Democracy, itself. As much as we value our freedoms and our ability to participate and to affect the political debate, it is that same freedom that requires consensus rather than coercion.

There are very few, if any, issues with which we as Americans can readily agree upon. Every single issue, large and small, becomes the subject of intense political debate. These debates often bring progress to a screeching halt. Indeed there are times when our system appears to be completely broken. Even when we are at our political best, progress moves at a snail-like pace.

As frustrating as this reality is to most Americans, it is an unfortunate byproduct of our freedom. Our system of government requires a majority consensus. Now, as we clearly understand on an individual level, it is extremely difficult to get two people to agree on a regular basis. So imagine the difficulty of finding a consensus among 310 million Americans.[41]

Our constitutional freedom is the very thing that allows for so much friction, disagreement, and painfully slow progress. For our nation to operate at an optimal speed and to accomplish the great things we are capable of accomplishing, the nation as a whole must mature to a level far beyond where we currently are. Progress in the United States requires that individuals have the ability to listen to someone with whom they vehemently disagree or to acknowledge the right of someone to advocate for that which they would oppose. Similarly, for us to continue to enjoy our religious freedom, we must recognize our fellow citizens' rights to worship as they choose, and their right not to worship at all. This is both the cost and protector of our freedom. *unless you're right.*

Now consider the alternative: imagine living in a nation that was progressing at lightning speeds, but the cost of this progress was the restriction of speech, religion, and political action. This is the case of China. The Chinese people are experiencing amazing economic growth but are still under the control of an authoritarian regime. Progress in China is easier to achieve in the absence of opposition.

Nevertheless, no matter how immature the political discourse in our country may be or how painfully slow we may progress, most of us would agree the American dilemma is preferable to a political system which uses force rather than consensus to govern.

Just as our individual freedoms allow us to live lifestyles that can become oppressive, collectively, our freedom to participate equally in the political discourse allows for an equally oppressive political process, filled with the type of rhetoric and spin that is the hallmark of American politics in the twenty-first century. Just as with the prodigal son, our freedom requires a level of maturity which recognizes that our greatness will only be found when we begin to behave like the mature body politic our founders knew would be necessary to maintain a democracy, despite our freedom to behave like political children.[42]

A Maturing Process

There comes a time in our lives when we realize that we need to mature. No matter how much our family and friends hope that the day would come sooner rather than later, it will only come when we make up our minds for ourselves. When that day comes, our drive to become the best person possible is far more effective than any rules and regulations others tried to force on us. Like the prodigal son, all we need is to "come to ourselves."

I imagine a day when the American polity has matured to the point where we no longer allow our tremendous freedom to hinder our progress; a day when we no longer need anger to drive our political action, or pundits to inform our decisions.

Oppressive Freedom

There is no doubting that, as a nation, we can grow further than we are. However, since this maturity cannot be forced, it is something the citizenry must desire and achieve on its own terms.

Freedom requires a level of maturity and discipline in order for it not to be abused by the free or preyed upon by the despot. The source of that maturity can be found in numerous places from religion to philosophy and beyond. As deceptively beneficial as it may appear to have a greater authority present that is capable of imposing this type of discipline and maturity by force, the Constitution of the United States is in line with biblical principles of individual freedom in that it gives us the liberty to discover this level of freedom on our own, or not.

In all things political and spiritual, we must understand the principle of Oppressive Freedom. As much as we may believe that America would be better if more people were Christian, the Constitution grants us the right to make that decision for ourselves. In fact, our Constitutional freedom ensures that we have the right to live completely outside of someone else's moral framework.

Although he was granted every liberty he desired, the Prodigal Son did not understand that he did not have to indulge in each of them. Likewise, as Christian Americans we do not have to participate or even condone every freedom available to us in the United States. While we may adamantly disagree with the many oppressive activities that American freedom allows, it is the maturity we derive from Christ that keeps us from falling and not the force of laws aimed at legislating morality.

Not only do we, as Americans, not have to live according to anyone's moral standards, the Constitution guarantees us the freedom not to have our personal morality measured by someone else's spiritual benchmarks. In other words, no one in America can be the spiritual judge of another. Furthermore, a holy lifestyle can only be accomplished through our individual choices and decisions, not through forced morality. In the absence of this *forced* morality, we as individuals—and as Americans—have the freedom to be oppressed; but most importantly, we have the freedom to be free.

·SECTION 1·
GOD'S POLITICS AND THE ISSUES

2.

GOD'S POLITICS:

HOW WOULD JESUS VOTE?

Dr. James Kennedy (1930-2007), former pastor of Coral Ridge Presbyterian church in Fort Lauderdale, Florida, wrote the book, *How Would Jesus Vote?*[43] Admittedly, he began his book with the same scripture with which I originally planned to begin this book: the story of Joshua at the Battle of Jericho.[44]

> When Joshua was by Jericho, he lifted up his eyes and looked, and behold, a man was standing before him with his drawn sword in his hand. And Joshua went to him and said to him, 'Are you for us, or for our adversaries?' And he said, 'No; but I am the commander of the army of the Lord. Now I have come.' And Joshua fell on his face to the earth and worshiped and said to him, 'What does my lord say to his servant?' (Joshua 5:13-14, ESV)[45]

Many pastors and theologians interpret this text in a similar manner. The fact that Joshua offered worship to this "man" and the "man" accepted the worship signifies that this was much more than a man. To accept worship, he had to be more than an angel. In fact, theologians agree that Joshua was speaking to the pre-incarnated Christ—Jesus in the form of an angel operating in the Old-Testament.

GOD IS NOT A REPUBLICAN

Joshua, being the bold leader that he always was, unknowingly approached the Son of God and asked whether He was for them or their adversaries. Christ did not directly answer Joshua's question but instead said, "No." The Amplified Bible translates no as neither. This Old Testament scripture gives us the answer to one of the biggest questions and misconceptions we have about God: "Is God on our side or theirs?" The answer is neither.

Dr. Kennedy extrapolated the essence of this scripture in the same manner. Political speaking, God is neither Democrat nor Republican. Neither party has a legitimate claim to God. He is not on either side. While there are few who would directly claim that God was a Republican, there are even fewer who would claim He was a Democrat.

Dr. Kennedy proceeded to discuss how he believed Jesus would vote issue by issue. Although he began the book by saying God is neither Republican nor Democrat, by the end of the book, Kennedy left the readers feeling as though Jesus would vote Republican because He would be anti-abortion and anti-gay marriage. By extension, Kennedy implies that if we want to be like Jesus and do what Jesus would do, then we too would vote against any politician that supported abortion and gay rights.

How Serious Christians Should Vote

Just before the 2008 elections, a passer-by dropped off a stack of pamphlets in the foyer of our church. It was entitled *A Voter's Guide for Serious Christians*.[46] This brief pamphlet, much like Kennedy's book, never endorsed any political party or candidate. It went as far as giving a disclaimer stating that it was not endorsing a particular party or candidate. Nevertheless, the pamphlet made a clear assertion that no serious Christian could ever vote for a candidate who supports gay and abortion rights.[47] While it also included a section opposing stem-cell research, euthanasia, and cloning, the emphasis was placed on the two most contentious topics.[48] Both the pamphlet and Dr. Kennedy's publication implied that these matters were primary to God and, therefore, should be primary to Christians.

For the authors of the small pamphlet, all other political issues—including war, social justice, and economics—were secondary and open for debate; however, the issues they highlighted were "non-negotiable." [49, 50] Dr. Kennedy's book went much further than this. He asserted that God was both pro-capitalism, pro-national security, and pro-defense. He went as far as to say that it was not the role of the federal government to assist the poor because it was the responsibility of churches and private charity.[51]

Despite the "non-endorsement" legal disclaimers, both publications suggested that *serious* Christians could only vote for Republican candidates because the Republican Party stands against the same things Jesus stood against and support the same things Jesus would support. Nevertheless, how do we know that abortion and homosexuality are more important to God than matters of justice, peace, poverty, and economic morality? This question is important when we consider that in order for Evangelical Christians to vote against gay-rights and abortion, they are often voting against legislation that would bring economic morality and in favor of the death penalty and the expansion of the US war machine.

How can we prioritize the importance of issues to God? Life and death are important to God. However, there is no biblical basis to believe that the abortion of millions of children every year is a greater sin to Him than the 30,000 children that die from hunger every day around the globe. Therefore, how can Christians turn a blind eye to these questions of morality only to focus on sexual morality?

Measuring Sin

Can we put a measure of importance to God? Would we do so based on the magnitude of a sin or atrocity? If that is the case, what of the millions of lives lost because of war—no matter how just that war may be? Are those lives any less important to God than any other life? How is it that we pick and choose which issues are relevant to God, and by extension, conclude that those are the issues for which we should base our vote? We cannot.

> But we are all as an unclean thing, and all our righteousness is as filthy rags; and we all do fade as a leaf; and our iniquities, like the wind, have taken us away. —Isaiah 64:6 (KJV) [52]

Many pastors and theologians disagree on whether all sin is equal. Scripture indeed implies that certain sins carry more guilt than others and cause more harm to our bodies.[53] These scriptures refer to the effect that sin has on us as individuals or on one another. The idea of *magnitudes of offense* is reflected in our society in that certain crimes carry harsher punishments. Indeed, not all crimes are the same.

However, in the eyes of God, all sin requires atonement. The very foundation of our faith is the atonement of our sins through the crucifixion of Christ Jesus. Therefore, regardless of what measurement mankind places on sin, every sin required Jesus' crucifixion. From little white lies to atrocities such as genocide, Christ's death was necessary for the atonement of all sin. So in God's eyes, all sin is equal in that the price that had to be paid for every one of them, big or small was His Son's blood at Calvary.

Theological Relevance

This brief theological discourse is necessary for two reasons. First, men have a tendency to categorize sin and assign magnitudes to them. In a religious context, this allows us to label someone else's offense as "blasphemous" or "abominations" with little regard for their own sin.

> Why do you see the speck that is in your brother's eye, but do not notice the log that is in your own eye? Or how can you say to your brother, 'Let me take the speck out of your eye,' when there is a log in your own eye? You hypocrite... —Matthew 7:3-5 (ESV) [54]

> There is not a righteous man on earth who does what is right and never sins.
> —Ecclesiastes 7:20 (NIV)

Second, if all sin is the same before God how can we assert that one moral issue is more important to Him than another? We cannot say with theological integrity that matters of abortion and homosexuality are of greater concern to God than economic exploitation, injustice, and oppression.[55] For years, we have allowed some politicians and pastors to focus all of the church's electoral energy to fight issues of social morality at the expense of economic morality. God is displeased with all sin and injustice; not just the ones that conveniently fit into the narrow definitions of the Republican Party.

WHAT DO WE WANT AS CHRISTIANS?

What do we want as Christians? If our goal is to bring morals to society, attempting to force these morals through legislation makes us no better than Muslim extremists who want to enforce Shari 'a Law. Do we want a nation in which sin is outlawed? If that is the case, are we ready to make all sin illegal? Perhaps we only wish to outlaw the sins that we do not commit. What is it that we want? Do we want a nation that forces morality on its citizens, even at the expense of our liberty to live life as we see fit? Are we looking to dominate the nation by force or do we wish to lift up Christ so that He would draw all men to him?

Now, consider if Christians lived lives that were more like Christ. Wouldn't the arrival of millions of true Christians be powerful enough to turn the world upside down?[56] Is it that the world is entirely too sinful, or is the real problem that there aren't enough Christians who truly are like Christ? For years, we have been told by ambitious pastors and political strategists that abortion and homosexuality are the foremost issues that Christians should oppose with our vote. These issues have been used election cycle after election cycle to elect Republicans into office. And to what end?

BAIT AND SWITCH

Surely America should be *more Christian* by now when we consider all of the Republican politicians elected with the evangelical vote. What meaningful progress has been made on the very issues that they have lifted up as preeminent? What has the Christian vote been used to accomplish if not morality?

After the election of Ronald Reagan in 1980, Jerry Falwell hailed the day as a triumphant victory for Christians. Falwell believed that the nation finally had a president who would help us return prayer to school, oppose abortion, and bring Christian values to the forefront.[57] Although a Constitutional Amendment to allow voluntary prayer in school was presented in Congress, it was categorically defeated in part because it had minimal political support from the White House.[58] That same year, Reagan appointed Sandra Day O'Conner to the Supreme Court. Though she had only cast one vote as a state legislator which was aimed at decriminalizing abortions, many Christians and "Right-to-Lifers" felt Reagan had betrayed them on an issue that was pivotal in mobilizing them behind his campaign.[59] In his initial reaction to the appointment of O'Conner, Jerry Falwell stated: "All good Christians should be concerned."[60, 61] By the end of Reagan's second term, it became apparent to the evangelical community that Reagan had taken them for granted. After eight years of broken promises and being marginalized the Evangelical community put their hopes into one of their own: Pat Robertson.[62]

Robertson entered the 1988 Presidential election as a Republican candidate. Hopes were high, and it seemed as though God Himself were moving on behalf of Christians nationwide when Robertson shocked the world by beating George H.W. Bush in the Iowa Primaries.[63] The momentary joy would not last. Evangelicals were dealt another disappointment after Bush decidedly defeated Robertson. Upon opening an inquiry into hate crimes against minorities, gays and lesbians, Evangelical Christians were infuriated when Bush invited representatives from the LGBT (Lesbian, Gay, Bisexual and Transgendered) to the White House. This was the first time Gay activists had ever been invited to the White House.[64]

At the end of President Bill Clinton's second term in 2000, evangelicals were once again mobilized and elected George W. Bush to the Presidency. Many believers felt that they had finally elected a President that not only believed as they did, but would be willing to enact policies based on that morality.[65] In fact, between 2000 and 2006, the Republican Party had their greatest opportunity to enact morality based legislation. The GOP controlled both houses of Congress, the White House, and a conservative leaning Supreme Court.

Despite their clear majority and advantage, no significant gains were made in overturning *Roe v. Wade*. The only accomplishments during this period were a series of bills which cut federal funding for abortions and state level restrictions. Evangelicals and pro-lifers watched their greatest opportunity in a generation to overturn *Roe v. Wade* fade away.

On issues of homosexuality, a half-hearted effort to amend the constitution to define marriage as being between a man and a woman died a quick legislative death. Politicians and analysts on both sides of the aisles knew that the gesture was merely symbolic and that it had no chance of passing even with a Republican majority in both houses of Congress.[66] The Bush Administration beckoned millions of Christian voters to stand with them in support of an amendment they knew had no possible chance of passing. It is no coincidence that President Bush announced his support of the Constitutional Amendment just one day after he launched his re-election campaign.[67]

The very presidents Christians helped to elect were enacting policies that directly opposed their religious interests. Christians had been mobilized to support the Republican ticket because it purported to represent family values, but in practice, Republicans operated no differently than Democrats.

In the last thirty years, the Republican Party has done little more than use social issues to rally the Christian vote. No Republican Administration elected by evangelicals delivered on the promises made to evangelicals. Which raises the question: Would a serious Christian continuously vote for politicians simply because they say Christian things yet do absolutely nothing to benefit their beliefs?

> For men shall be lovers of their own-selves... trucebreakers, false accusers...despisers of those that are good, traitors ... Having a form of godliness, but denying the power thereof: from such turn away. —2 Timothy 3:2-5 (KJV)[68]

Insult to Injury

Many Evangelical Christians feel that the Republican Party is their political home because of the party's public opposition to abortion and gay marriages. Sadly, the Republican Party establishment has very little respect for the Christian community. From the beginning of the merger of the GOP and Evangelicals in 1980 through today, the Establishment treats Evangelicals as a necessary evil needed to gain political power. This is evident by the manner in which they speak of Evangeli-

God's Politics

cals, the lack of political progress on their behalf, and general lack of respect.

In response to Jerry Falwell's comment stating that every good Christian should be concerned with President Reagan's nomination of Sandra Day O'Conner to the Supreme Court, Republican icon, Barry Goldwater, stated:

> Every good Christian should line up and kick Falwell's ass.[69]

A generation later, Republican political commentator, Tucker Carlson, spoke openly with liberal commentator, Chris Matthews, on his perception of the true relationship between the party and Evangelicals:

Carlson: The deep truth is that the elites in the Republican Party have pure contempt for the evangelicals who put their party in power.

Matthews: How do you know that? How do you know that?

Carlson: Because I know them. Because I grew up with them, because I live with them. They live on my street. Because I live in Washington, and I know that everybody in our world has contempt for the evangelicals...

Matthews: So this gay marriage issue and other issues...are simply tools to get elected?

Carlson: That's exactly right. It's pandering to the base in the most cynical way, and the base is beginning to figure it out.[70]

A Sobering Truth

The truth is often difficult to hear and, at times, even more difficult to accept. The truth is, the Republican Party has done little to change the very issues they have used to mobilize the

45

Christian vote. The reason for their failures is equally troubling as their lack of results. One thing must be true: either the Republican Party believes that it is not in their best interest to implement Christian policies with the political power they gained from Christian voters, or the reason for their failure is that the Republican Party is unable to enact Christian policies despite continued promises to do so.

Why would it not in their best interest? Consider if the Republicans were able to make good on their promises to outlaw abortions and ban same-sex marriage in perpetuity. With a victory of this magnitude, there would be little left to rally Christians during election cycles. Without the power of moral rhetoric to mobilize Christian voters around, the Republican Party would lose the significant voting power that Evangelicals bring to the polls every election cycle. The Republican Party has every incentive to prolong bringing resolution to these matters because it allows them to stir the emotions of Evangelicals during election years.

If Republicans truly wanted to affect moral change, could they? The Constitution guarantees freedom and liberty for every American. Religious freedoms ensure every citizen the right to worship as they see fit. It also ensures them the right not to worship at all. Imposing Christian based legislation infringes on the rights of Americans who wish to live their lives outside of the influence of religion. Few politicians—and even fewer Supreme Court Justices—would vote to send our nation down the slippery slope of taking away freedoms from Americans. Therefore, Republican promises have been, and will continue to be, empty if those promises require infringement of rights.

The Dilemma of Free Will

The dilemma that we face as Christians is accepting the fact that God—just as America—allows us to be free and to live our lives as we see fit. It is biblically true that God will not force any of us to serve Him nor live a holy life. It is a choice that we must make.[71] Furthermore, He does not force anyone to become a Christian or to be saved.[72] All that we do for Him must be done by our own free will.

If we attempt to regulate the morality of a nation, or attempt to legislate holiness, our efforts would never be acceptable in the eyes of God because the resulting obedience would be the product of compulsion and not of our own desire. Therefore, no amount of legislation will make our society more pleasing in God's eyes if that legislation forces people to live in a manner contrary to their free will. We must freely choose to live as He desires.

Millions of laws are now in our legal code, yet those laws are incapable of creating a biblically moral or holy society. The unrepentant serial killer does not receive salvation simply because the legal system imprisoned him. The unrepentant thief does not receive salvation because imprisonment keeps him from stealing. Legislated morality only serves to prohibit the desired actions of the individuals the legal system is able to catch. It does not necessarily change their hearts or desires.

> [Thomas] Aquinas[73] explains that human law is unable to direct the interior acts of a man's soul. As a result, human law has a difficult time directing people toward the path of virtue, since genuine human goodness depends not only on external actions but upon interior movements of the soul, which are hidden…[74]

If abortions became illegal, it would merely stop all legal abortions. Some women would still desire and seek out illegal abortions. If homosexuality were outlawed, it would not change the fact that a segment of our society has desires for the same-sex. Outlawing either will not make America a more Christian nation. Imprisoning doctors who perform abortions, women that receive them, or gays and lesbians will not make America more pleasing in God's eyes. It would only be pleasing in the eyes of those who are fixated with sexual morality.

> And if it is evil in your eyes to serve the Lord, choose this day whom you will serve...as for me and my house, we will serve the Lord."
> —Joshua 24:15 (ESV)

The preceding scripture demonstrates the individual's responsibility to live a life that pleases God. God does not force holiness on us.[75] If God, the almighty creator, gives us the right to choose how we live our lives and to make our own decisions in regards to Him, who are we to force our fellow man to live the way we think is best? What right do we have to force our moral standards on someone regardless if we believe those standards are beneficial to them? The answer is simple: we have no right. While our charge as Christians is to tell a dying world about the saving power of Christ, God has not given us the authority or the ability to force them to comply.

As Christians, we should be the first to live the lives that we preach about to others. Our lives should be the example that other men and women see. The way we live is meant to be the drawing force that compels people to come to Christ, not forced coercion through politics and legislation,

How Should Christians Vote?

Christianity has been manipulated and mislead by political strategists from all parties. The Republican Party is not the only culprit. However, over the past thirty years it has been asserted that in order to be a good Christian, one must vote with the Republican Party. This is both logically and theologically erroneous.

No matter how honest and sincere the intentions of leaders such as James Robison, Pat Robertson, James Kennedy, and Jerry Falwell were, the result of their actions is still the same: Christians have been delivered into the hands of men and women who have made promises on issues that they have no intention or ability to change. Republicans have gotten the Evangelical vote in the name of Christ, and won victories in the name of their economic policies.

This does not make the Republican Party evil or nefarious. This is simply what political parties do. Their entire reason for existing is to secure a large enough coalition to obtain political power for the purposes of achieving their political goals. For the last thirty years, the Republican Party's most important constituencies have been Evangelical Christians and Pro-Life voters. Sadly, time has proven that the Party has failed to deliver on any of their promises in meaningful ways. Furthermore, they have insisted that the nation stay focused on matters which conveniently have no repercussions on their economic platform while turning a blind eye to matters of economic morality—which are also important to God.

How Would Jesus Vote?

It is impossible to answer the question of how Jesus would vote. One thing is certain; He was too wise to be misled by politicians offering mere lip service. He would not allow himself to be pigeonholed by the false dichotomies that modern politics present to us as choices. He would not sacrifice justice and equality for the sake of morality, nor would he sacrifice morality for the sake of justice. If we are ever to be like him, we can no longer fall into these snares.

We must vote with wisdom and begin to see the truth behind the rhetoric. The bait that political parties have lifted up for Christians to rally behind has only been a distraction. Republicans have been getting the Christian vote based on moral issues that they have no intention or ability of changing. This type of behavior exists in both the Democratic and Republican Parties. It exists in all facets of politics. This is the nature of politics. Some politicians will say and do anything in order to get our vote. Republicans just do it in Jesus' name.

3.

MISSED OPPORTUNITIES:

THE PRO-LIFE AND PRO-CHOICE DEBATE

It was the final semester in my master's program at Florida Atlantic University. Spring time in South Florida is usually a tossup between extremely beautiful and extremely rainy. That day was beautiful. As I took my normal route from the parking garage across campus and to the graduate assistants' offices, I began to see enormous displays in the center of the main courtyard. From a distance, I could not make out what the images were, but I could see that a large crowd had gathered around them.

As I drew nearer and began to make out what the images were, I found myself instantly infuriated. My peaceful daily walk across campus was interrupted by towering images of babies that had been aborted. Pictures of torn and tattered fetuses filled the entire courtyard as demonstrators began to assemble on the opposite side of the barricades which were erected out of necessity. I took note of the police officers that were patrolling an area which was normally quite serene. This day's beauty, however, was interrupted by a pro-life demonstration.

Then I remembered my anger. I stopped counting the number of armed police officers, turned my attention back towards the gruesome images, and remembered my anger. "Why do I have to look at this?" I thought to myself. I remember asking myself why I had to see the fractured skulls and severed hands of unborn children that were so tiny they had to be measured against a George Washington quarter for perspective.

My wife and I had just celebrated the birth of our son no more than two months before this. Eight months prior to his birth, I saw his heartbeat flickering and thought to myself, "That's my boy," long before I knew whether he would be healthy, happy, or even a boy or a girl. It was nothing more than a flickering light, but I remember how strong it was beating. To me, he was already living.

Seeing the images of what an aborted child looked like triggered a visceral response that I did not fully understand. Who was I angry at? Why was I angry? Was I upset because the pro-life demonstrators had invaded my personal space, or was I angered by the realities of abortion? Anger without knowledge is counterproductive, so I stood there staring at the images taking it all in, hoping to understand the emotions I felt.

It did not take long. After a few moments of reflection, I understood why I was angry. The anger I felt was an outgrowth of the sorrow I felt from looking at the images of abortions. My heart was broken for the millions of children that would never be born and because of how horrifically their lives were aborted. Then, I considered what my life would be like without my son. The thought did not last longer than a brief moment before my mind completely rejected it, refusing to entertain it. I attempted to comprehend my sorrow multiplied by the millions of children aborted each year in the United States. "Effective technique," I thought to myself. They had my attention, but most of all my heart.

I began to look at the presentation with a new set of eyes, taking in all of the grotesqueries of abortions while being thankful every minute for my son and silently shedding a tear for such a tremendous loss. As I walked around the presentation, I could overhear small debates between the organizers and students. There was no need for me to get involved in those arguments because the truth of the nature of abortions was displayed in front of me on the billboards. There was no debating what my eyes saw. Then, at the very end of the exhibition was a final life-sized display. This poster was not of an aborted fetus but, rather, of President Obama and his family. The phrase, "President Obama's policies support the murder of innocent children," juxtaposed Sasha and Malia's smiling faces as a contrast to the images of the aborted children. In an instant, all of the effectiveness and weight of their message was lost because of their politics.

Self-Sabotage

That day I realized a fundamental truth that the pro-life movement must become aware of with: personal politics do not matter when confronted with the grim realities of abortion. The demonstrators had the attention of nearly every person that walked by. No one could deny that what we were seeing was far more than tragic: it was an atrocity. However, the moment the demonstrators inserted partisan politics into the discussion, lines were drawn in the sand. The moment that issues of women's rights began to be debated, passion and tempers began to flare. The effectiveness of the display had the potential of changing the heart of someone considering abortion. All of that effectiveness was unnecessarily lost.

What good did it do to include a poster of Barack Obama in their anti-abortion demonstration? Why was it necessary to insert politics into the discussion? The images were undeniable. Politics only served to weaken the power of the meaningful moment the pro-life advocates created. Why would the demonstrators sabotage their own efforts with politics?

To answer this question we have to examine the goals of the demonstrators. Was their goal to sway the opinions of people in hopes of reducing the number of abortions? If this is the case, the demonstrators inadvertently or, perhaps, unwittingly sabotaged their own efforts. More people were upset at the demonstrators than they were at the demonstration. This was evident by the "free-speech" wall that the university placed directly across from the demonstration. It was nothing more than a bulletin board the school hastily erected to give students the chance to respond to the demonstration. Phrases such as "No politician will ever tell me what to do with my body," and "My body, my rights" littered the board from top to bottom. Each of these phrases surrounded an expletive written so boldly it was nearly as visible as the demonstrators' billboards. No. If their goal was to win the hearts and minds of students faced with a decision between *Life* and *Rights*, then the demonstrators failed.

I stepped back far enough to see the entire display so that I could digest the larger message and not just the individual billboards. Then I realized the reason for President Obama's billboard being the last image in the display. I realized, somehow they wanted to link the visceral anger I felt to the President and his political party. Perhaps the demonstrators believed the images would make us upset enough to vote President Obama and all of the other Democrats out of office. If this was their goal, then they failed again. It only served as the impetus I needed to engage in the debate.

"Excuse me." I politely interrupted one demonstrator's conversations and asked, "Who is in charge here?" One of the workers gestured towards a scruffy, bearded gentleman climbing down from setting up the final billboard. As he came down, the worker spoke to him and gestured in my direction. After we cordially shook hands, I introduced myself and began:

> Why was it necessary for you to inject President Obama into a discussion that we could otherwise agree on? You had me until that point. Can't you see how your politics are undermining all of your efforts here?

He paused for a second, perhaps in order to customize his response for whoever he observed me to be. Then he began to explain how he believed that Obama's support of women's rights ultimately translated into support for abortions. "Perhaps," I told him.

> But if your goal is to convince someone out here not get an abortion, can't you see how politicizing the conversation would cause them to turn them away? I mean, I'm a father. These billboards spoke to me loud and clear. But once I saw your political angle, I stopped listening.

Out of the corner of my eye, I could see a young woman in her early twenties quickly approaching our conversation with an intrigued look on her face. I presume she was so anxious to weigh in on our conversation that she couldn't wait until she got face-to-face with me; rather, she began to speak as she approached. "We don't support any political party. We are simply highlighting the fact that President Obama's policies support the murder of innocent children. He supports the woman's right to choose; we support the child's right to live."

"It's that simple, huh?" I thought to myself. She was still talking, but her words were muffled out by my thoughts. Admittedly, they were thoughts that she inspired. She framed the conversation so simply by saying they were pro-life, and Obama was pro-choice. I guess I had to pick a side. Either I was for taking away women's rights or I was for killing the innocent.

False Dichotomy

So many times we are asked to choose which side we are on, either Life or Choice. Not only with abortion, but this is also true with so many other things in life. It seems life has become more about choosing sides than understanding the other side. As if being in a situation like this isn't difficult enough, we have to add into the mix the fact that we are Christian. How can we as Christians do anything but support the pro-life movement? And if we support the pro-life movement, how could we ever vote for a Democrat?

We have been asked these questions at some point in our lives. But what do we do when it is slammed in our faces by demonstrators? What do we do when our pastor or bishop preaches about it? How are we to deal with the pressures of being a Christian but voting for someone who supports *Choice* over *Life*? How many Christians have felt a religious obligation to cast their vote to protect the lives of the innocent while silently confused because we also support the privacy of a woman and her sacred freedom to have control over her body? If we violate the rights of women, wouldn't we be violating all of our rights?

In that moment, as the young lady ranted about how I could not be a Christian and be pro-choice, I realized how wrong she was: I realized how wrong all of us have been. Our faith does not mandate that we choose between supporting abortion and supporting women's· rights, as if there were no other ground for us to stand. Clearly, I was in favor of life. My son was alive from the moment I first saw his heart beating. However, it was equally clear to me that the government had no right to infringe on a woman's privacy in regards to what she does with her body. All of this time both sides have been trying to force us choose sides, and most of us scramble either to the left or to the right and then harden our positions.

That was when I realized the truth: I was both pro-life and pro-choice. I hated to see the images of slaughtered children. Anyone, on either side of the argument, should be able to see that the number of abortions performed in the United States every year is both atrocious and ridiculous.[76] Yet, in that very moment, when my political belief was challenged by my love for life, I still believed that a woman should have the right to make decisions about her personal life as freely as I can make decisions about my own. No politician or demonstrator has a right to infringe on a woman's rights if for no other reason than the fact that we (men) would never allow the government to infringe on ours.

How was I going to reconcile this position? Slowly her words became audible to me again as I rejoined the conversation just in time to hear her ask me:

"So are you pro-choice or are you pro-life?"

"I'm both."

Tension Resolved

It is so much easier to see things through the eyes of absolutes: either black and white or left and right. Struggling with choices that seem like contradictions can cause your head to hurt, but sometimes a subject is important enough to endure the discomfort of living in the gray. We churchgoers have the biggest dose of this problem. Maybe it is because religious matters are so absolute that we inadvertently carry it over to every other aspect of our lives and society. "It's heaven or hell." "You're either saved or you're not."

Life must be about resolving contradictions, and Christians are especially equipped to do so whether we know it or not. How else could we have hope when a situation is hopeless? How else could we believe in God when we have no tangible evidence?[77]

I could see the passion in the young woman's eyes. Her voice quivered as she searched for something that could convince me that abortions were wrong and should be illegal. What she did not realize was that she did not need to convince me that abortions were horrible; I already knew it for myself. If my personal convictions were not enough, the billboards of slaughtered children surely convinced me.

However, what she could not convince me of was her premise that, as a Christian, I could never vote for anyone who is pro-choice even though the politicians who profess to be pro-life have yet to accomplish any significant or meaningful victories for the cause of life.

"What great accomplishments have Republicans delivered for the cause of life?" My question interrupted her. She had been talking the entire time I was thinking. She looked somewhat dazed by the question. I continued, "If anyone should be up here on display it should be George W. Bush and the Republican Party because they have used your movement for political gain, yet they haven't delivered any major victories for your cause." She hesitated. Now I had her attention.

The scruffy gentleman in charge chimed in by explaining, as though I didn't already know: "Yeah, but Bush is no longer in office. Obama is."

The Party of Life?

President Obama and the Democratic Party would have to bear the brunt of the demonstration because their Party was in power. If any party were culpable for abortions in our nation, wouldn't it be the Republican Party? I wondered if the demonstrators knew that *Roe v. Wade* was decided by a Republican appointed Supreme Court.[78] Of the two dissenting voices, Justice Byron White and Justice William Rehnquist, White had been appointed by a Democrat.[79] Did they know that despite Republicans having their greatest opportunity in over thirty years to challenge the decision, *Roe v. Wade* still stands?

Between 2000 and 2006, all branches of the federal government were in the hands of the GOP. The White House, Senate, and House of Representatives were all controlled by the Republican Party while the Supreme Court had a conservative leaning. If significant gains were ever to be made on behalf of the pro-life movement, they would have been made during this period of time.

The movement helped to elect enough Republicans in office that the party controlled all branches of the government, and yet the Republican Party did not gain any significant ground for the cause of Life. In the generations since *Roe v. Wade*, the GOP has only provided token victories in the form of cutting federal funds, and imposing various restrictions and stipulations. But abortions still go on. Although many would claim that it is the Democratic Party and the pro-choice movement that is to blame, surely the Republican Party could have accomplished more in thirty years than budget cuts if they were willing and able. In spite of all of their "efforts," abortions decreased at a faster rate under the Clinton administration than the Bush administration.[80]

Personhood Laws define conception as the beginning of life. This is the most aggressive movement to end abortion in the nation. The law effectively make all abortions murder. This, subsequently, makes abortion and some forms of birth control illegal. As aggressive as this movement may appear, the electorates in many states—including states as conservative as Mississippi—have rejected these initiatives. Despite all of the restrictions, impediments to access, and defunding of abortion programs the overall rate of abortions decreased only eight-percent during the Bush administration. Over 1.2 million abortions were performed each year between 2000 and 2008.[81]

The Republican Party has failed on the issue of abortion. It is vitally important that we understand the reasons why the Party has failed. Was it because Republicans could not do anything significant for the pro-life movement, or because they simply chose not to do anything significant? Again, the answer is both. *Roe v. Wade* is the law of the land. Until there is a legal challenge that reaches the Supreme Court, Congress can only provide token victories in the form of cutting federal aid to organizations that perform abortions. Republicans on the state level have been able to make abortions more difficult; however, they have not been able to end them.

Suppose the GOP could overturn *Roe v. Wade* and make abortions illegal. Would they not lose one of their most fierce support groups? This is not because pro-life advocates would turn away from the Republican Party; rather, because there would no longer be a cause for mobilization. The attainment of the specific goals which served as the driving force behind a movement often has the effect of lessening the ability to be mobilized. The pro-life movement has moved millions of voters to the polls on behalf of the Republican Party for over thirty years. The GOP cannot strategically afford to lose that mobilizing force.[82]

Demand for Abortions

The underlying problem with abortions is not the availability or ease of access to abortions. During the time in our nation's history when abortions were illegal in most states, many women obtained illegal abortions. Indeed, the legalization of abortions was, in many respects, a direct response to the number of women that were dying from illegal procedures.[83]

This historical fact, coupled with the inability of current restrictive legislation to produce meaningful decreases in the abortion rate suggests a harsh reality: illegal or not, if a woman feels she needs an abortion she will go through whatever bureaucratic barricades necessary to obtain one. So then, we must understand that the problem of abortion cannot be fixed by restricting the supply and ease of access to abortions: it can only be fixed by addressing the reasons demand for abortions exists.

The marriage between the pro-life movement and the Republican Party has truly only been beneficial to the GOP. Sadly, this union has been detrimental to the cause of Life. This is evident by the demonstration that day. Though the pro-life demonstration had both the attention and the hearts of everyone who saw the images, they lost both because they mixed an invaluable message with their political allegiance to the Republican Party. Perhaps they didn't think they were endorsing a political group. Maybe they honestly thought that

Missed Opportunities

it was the right thing to do to place a picture of President Obama at the end of the presentation in hopes of making sure everyone knows he was pro-choice. Regardless, politicizing their message has not benefited their cause. From the responses plastered on the Free Speech wall on campus that day, the very people who needed to hear the message were turned off because of the politics of abortion. How much clearer could we have all heard the pro-life message if it had not been distorted by political rhetoric?

The Manipulation of a Worthy Movement

Pro-life advocates have been politically taken advantage of like so many other groups. The amount of time, energy, and care it took to organize a demonstration of the magnitude they presented on our campus that day was evident. Obviously, this group was passionate about saving the lives of the unborn.

However, when political lines are drawn in the sand, we find that both sides begin to demonize the other and few, if any, are able to hear what the other side has to say. The core reason for the pro-life movement is without question a worthy cause. They have relentlessly stood to bring an end to the thousands of abortions that occur every day. Anyone who has ever had a child, wanted a child, or seen the grim reality of what we, as a nation, are doing to our children must admit that theirs is a noble cause. Unfortunately, they have focused their efforts in the wrong direction. Instead of addressing the underlying reasons that women obtain abortions, the pro-life movement has been fighting a losing political battle to remove a woman's right to obtain one.

Unfortunately, while the pro-life movement has helped to elect representatives, senators, governors, and even presidents, there are still over one million abortions performed annually in the United States. Abortions have not ended. What has ended is federal funding for thousands of programs that would support women during and after pregnancy: the very programs that would help the hard-working mother who has no healthcare to be able to get the prenatal care she needs to have a healthy baby. Funding has been cut for after-school programs, leaving many working parents with few options for childcare. Funding has been cut for contraception for the very poorest among us—those that disproportionately obtain abortions.[84] [85]

The very social programs designed to foster stronger communities and families which would help to decrease the need and the demand for abortions are the only things that have ended under Republican leadership while abortions remain legal. Pro-life advocates have worked countless hours and donated millions of dollars to the Republican Party who, in turn, has done little for their cause.

Is God Opposed to Abortions?

Some people in the debate feel the need to argue that the Bible does not specifically mention abortion. The subsequent argument is that, because of this, we cannot categorize abortion as sin. However, when we see the gruesome nature of abortion, it is difficult to believe that God would condone the act. Regardless of whether we categorize abortions as sin or not, it does not change the reality of abortions in America. Over one-million abortions are performed in the U.S. annually. Labeling this a tragedy is an understatement. The biggest failing of the Pro-Choice movement and the Democratic Party is their inability to convey the message that a person who is pro-choice is not pro-abortion. It is not the morality of abortions which needs defending: it is the rights of women that need defending. There is a significant difference.

Nevertheless, God does not force us to live according to His Word. He does not compel us to be saved, nor does he force us not to sin. God has given us the right to choose.[86] This is not to say that He endorses the pro-choice movement, but it is to say that He gives us the liberty to decide whether we want to serve and obey Him, or even if we want to believe in Him. He does not force His will on us. Not only this, but He gives us the right to choose how we want to live our lives. Surely there comes great responsibilities with such freedom, but the fact that He gives us this freedom should translate to every aspect of our lives.[87] If God gives us this freedom, then who are we to take it away from someone else?

The Church has preached against abortions for many years to no avail. Labeling abortion as a sin has not helped to decrease the number of performed in America. In many respects, the argument over the sin distinction of abortions is not one worth having. What we should be debating is how we can address the demand for abortions so that we can see meaningful decreases.

What of Sexual Morality?

As believers, we should teach abstinence because it is in line with our faith. But truthfully, abstinence alone has not worked and likely never will. It most certainly has not worked inside of the Christian community. Sixty-five percent of abortions in the United States are performed on Christian patients.[88] Think about that. If we as Christians could ever get our own houses in order, we could see a decline in abortions by sixty-five percent. What an amazing victory this would be for the cause of Life!

Bringing Ourselves into Subjection

In regards to sexual morality, I am loathed to bring up the most glaring hypocrisy in the Body of Christ. Nevertheless, from one Christian to another, how can we lecture society about living sexually moral lives when our congregations and leadership are replete with disgusting examples of sexual immorality? It is so rampant that there is no need to list the names of pastors who have been caught in adultery, bishops who've molested young boys, and leaders who preached against homosexuality only to be exposed as being gay themselves.[89] Divorce rates in the church are just as high as outside of the church.[90] So what moral example can we ever set for society when what goes on in our churches is just as bad as, if not far worse than, what goes on in the world? We need a revival: not a national revival to tell America what it is doing wrong, but a revival in our churches so we can begin to practice what we preach.

The Third Way

The GOP had their best opportunity to mount a serious challenge to *Roe v. Wade* between 2000 and 2006 and did little more than give the pro-life movement token victories on the federal and the state levels. If the Republican Party truly wanted to see an end to abortions, they would do more than offer false overtures of making abortions illegal. They would make policies which targeted the demand for abortions and not just the supply of abortions.

As Christians, we believe that when God fixes something He doesn't treat the symptoms; he cures the underlying causes. Policies that would decrease the poverty rate would surely decrease the number of abortions. Programs that would provide resources to families that need childcare would decrease the demand for abortions. However, politicians on the Right only seem to stir up the passion and anger of Christians in time for elections. The pro-life movement fights year round to save the lives of the unborn only to have typical politicians patronize them just in time for elections. They deserve better than this.

What needs to replace the abusive relationship between the pro-life movement and the Republican Party is a meaningful partnership between the pro-life and pro-choice movements. No one would dare say that they want to see the rate of abortions increase; therefore, a concrete strategy, aimed at seeing a decline in abortions, should be created. This can be accomplished, not by attacking a woman's right over her body, but by attacking the underlying causes and reasons women obtain abortions. The pro-life movement would need to move away from policies that encroach on women's rights and pro-choice advocates would need to understand, and make clear, that maintaining choice does not require maintaining abortions at the current level.

The pro-life movement has a passion and a zeal that can benefit every American. Imagine if they were to move in harmony with the pro-choice movement to address the underlying causes of abortions with the express intentions of seeing annual reductions. In addition to seeing a decline in the number of abortions, we would also see a decline in poverty rates.[91]

All of this time we have been fighting against each other while the best solution existed in the nexus of disagreements. If we are ever to find these solutions, we must be able to listen to each other even when we disagree with each other. Real world solutions rarely exist in the comforts of absolutes.[92] They often reside in the discomforts of a compromise. We will never be able to listen to each other long enough to find these solutions unless we first identify and remove the distractions that have divided us for generations.

Same Debate, Different Day

I left the demonstration and made my way to the class I was scheduled to teach that morning. As much as I wish I could tell you that the young woman and I came to some type of resolution, we didn't. We walked away with no resolution because we did not take the time needed to weed out enough political distractions to learn about our respective viewpoints. All we had time to do was to argue our side of the debate. It was *that* argument—the same argument that goes on every day in America—which caused us to miss out on the solution that was right in front of us the entire time: working together. And just as with so many other conversations and debates about abortion around the country, another opportunity for progress was lost.

4.

GAY RIGHTS AND MARRIAGE EQUALITY

One of the pillars of the Republican Party platform has been the assertion of the traditional definition of marriage. Christians define marriage to be a union between a man and a woman. The Republican platform has included fierce opposition to same-sex couples obtaining the legal rights attached to marriage, also known as marriage equality. This position has served the Republican Party well. There are very few issues that drive Christians to the polls more than opposition of same-sex marriage. The issue is brought forward just before every election in time to rally the Evangelical vote.

While the Republican Party has willingly used this issue to get the votes of socially conservative Christians, many members of the Party understand that there is little that can be done to stop same-sex couples from eventually gaining equal access and treatment under the law. Despite the opposition of Evangelical leaders, the Republican Party has begun to welcome gay rights advocacy groups into the conservative coalition. Groups such as GOProud and the Log Cabin Republicans have been incorporated into the same coalition with Evangelicals who oppose same-sex marriage.

GOD IS NOT A REPUBLICAN

What God Hates and Abominations

Christian opposition to gay and lesbian rights—marriage equality being preeminent among them—is the result of the interpretation of scripture that suggests that God hates homosexuality and considers it to be an abomination. Many traditional Christians consider homosexuality to be a sin, in a special category of its own. The self-righteousness of sin comparisons sets in as some Christians point to the word "abomination" found in Leviticus 20, and use it to assert that God hates homosexuals, and that homosexuality is a sin greater than other transgressions:

> If a man lies with a male as with a woman, both of them have committed an abomination; they shall surely be put to death; their blood is upon them.—Leviticus 20:13 (ESV)

Many Christians fail to realize, while we are condemning gays and lesbians, we are inadvertently condemning ourselves. Either we forgot to continue reading, or we chose to ignore the other things that the Bible reveals that God hates and considers abominations:

> These six things the Lord hates, indeed, seven are an abomination to Him. A proud look, a lying tongue, and hands that shed innocent blood. A heart that deviseth wicked imaginations, feet that be swift in running to mischief, a false witness that speaketh lies, and he that soweth discord among the brethren.

With this scripture, God made sure not to leave anyone out of the category of "sinners" that commit the various abominations that He hates. Furthermore, anyone who believes that they have never committed one of these transgressions is already guilty of the second. Therefore, we should not be so quick to lift homosexuality as the only sin that God hates; indeed, there are many more that fall into the same category.

COURTHOUSE OR GOD'S HOUSE?

My wife and I had two weddings. The first was at the county courthouse. Because we lived over two hours apart, it made more financial sense for us to move in together before our wedding date. So we would not be "living in sin," we were married by the Justice of the Peace in a courtroom designed to resemble a church. Our church ceremony followed two months later. Shortly after the courthouse ceremony, we realized that although our marriage license meant we were married in the eyes of the law, neither of us felt it was official until we had our church ceremony. We wanted our ceremony to be in the sight of God. Admittedly, our Christian logic was flawed:

> The eyes of the Lord are in every place, beholding the evil and the good. —Proverbs 15:3 (KJV)

God was just as present in the courthouse as He was in the sanctuary. Nevertheless, this was our personal belief, and it carried significant meaning to us. We felt we still needed God's blessings.

It was then that I finally understood the difference for me personally. For my wife and me, our marriage was not based on a piece of paper the government gave us. Our marriage was based on God's blessings. Although we had the legal rights that the government granted after our courthouse wedding, it still did not matter. Marriage was not so much a legal matter for us as it was a spiritual one.

WHO ORDAINS MARRIAGES: GOVERNMENT OR GOD

As Christians, do we believe that we are married because the government gave us a license, or because God recognizes and blesses our union? This is an important distinction and a vitally important question. If we, as Christians, believe that marriage is a product of the government, then opposition to same-sex marriages cannot be based on personal, religious beliefs. We violate the religious freedoms of other citizens if the justification for refusing marriage-equality is based on religious beliefs. The government has no constitutional right to delineate citizens' rights based on another groups' religious beliefs.

However, if we believe that God ordains marriages, then the entire debate becomes a religious one. If marriage is a spiritual and religious union for Christians, then the government should not be involved in determining who can or cannot be married: individual religions would make that determination. This would ultimately mean that the government would not recognize or prohibit any marriage because marriage itself would be deemed a religious institution.[93] Furthermore, because religions cannot grant legal rights, the government would have to determine another basis for granting the many rights it currently bestows on marriages.

The current reality is, marriage is a legal institution for all citizens and a religious institution for those citizens who adhere to religion. But the fact should be clear, no religious definition of marriage—which is interpreted differently even by every faith—should be able to dictate the *legal* definition of marriage any more than the government should be able to dictate the religious definition of marriage. Our personal and collective religious beliefs may influence the national dialogue and even government policy; however, based on the Constitution, those beliefs cannot be the sole basis for policy.

What is the Government's Role in Marriage?

The government's role in regulating marriage varies state by state and is minimal in comparison to the rights it grants for marriage. For instance, in some states, blood tests are required before receiving a marriage license. In other states, this is not the case. In general, the government grants new legal rights to married couples that they otherwise would not be entitled to receive. These legal rights also vary by state.

On the federal level, there are many rights granted to married couples including joint filing of tax returns, federal employee spousal insurance coverage, and Social Security survivors' benefit. According to the General Accounting Office there are approximately 1,138 rights and benefits that are bestowed on married couples.[94] Overwhelmingly, the government's greatest role in marriage is the conferring legal rights upon unions and not the regulation of unions. Notable exceptions are polygamy, underage marriage, and, of course, same-sex marriage.

THE DEFENSE OF MARRIAGE ACT

In 1996, Democratic President Bill Clinton signed into law the Defense of Marriage Act (DOMA). For federal purposes, this act defined marriage as being a union between a man and a woman. It also established a new policy that no state government had an obligation to recognize another state's definition of marriage. This law instantly took away all of the federal rights of gay spouses.[95] As stated above, this included approximately 1,100 rights. This action by a Democratic President may come as a surprise to many Christians. In fact, the greatest victory traditional marriage advocates ever received was at the hands of a Democrat and not a Republican.[96]

DOMA has since been deemed unconstitutional by a federal circuit judge and, subsequently, no longer enforced by the Obama Administration.[97] While the issue is far from resolved, this decision highlights the reality of the expansion of American rights: over time, rights will be realized if they fall within the framework of the Constitution. Unless policymakers derive a legitimate, non-religious justification for withholding legal rights from same-sex unions, marriage equality will be the inevitable outcome of American freedom.

EXAMINING OURSELVES

As with anything else, Christians must be clear about what we are seeking. Without clarity, we will continue to keep a multitude of rights away from a segment of society with no apparent goal in sight. Beyond the question of same-sex marriage, what are we really asking of the government with regard to homosexuality?

First, we must ask ourselves is, "Are we seeking to outlaw homosexuality?" Only the most extreme zealot would answer this in the affirmative. Many Christians would never assert that homosexuality should be illegal because we understand that we have all sinned and fallen short of God's glory.[98] If we attempt to make something illegal because we believe it is a sin, we must make all sin illegal, including those we secretly indulge.

Second, we must ask, "Is our goal to stop gays and lesbians from being gay and lesbian?" If this is the goal of some Christians, common sense dictates that denying same-sex couples marriage equality will not change their orientation. All it accomplishes is the perpetuation of second-class citizenship status for our fellow American citizens. If our goal is to force gays and lesbians into seclusion with a "lesser" citizenship, then we are not operating in the spirit of America nor the spirit of Christ but, rather, the spirit of bigotry.

Finally, we must ask ourselves, "If we are not seeking to make homosexuality illegal, nor attempting to change their orientation through legislation, what, then, is accomplished by denying marriage-equality?" Keeping same-sex couples from having the same access to the legal rights attached to marriage will not make America more Christian. Likewise, opposing their access to marriage-equality does not make us more Christian. Our faith is defined by what we do and believe as individuals and not by what we make others do—or restrict them from doing—by force.

Gay Rights and Marriage Equality

THE APPEARANCE OF NORMALITY

==Whether we know it or not, we as Christians are asking the government to maintain an appearance of normality. This is to say, we want the government to help maintain a certain societal image based on what we have determined to be normal, acceptable, and traditional.== Because it is impossible to make a person "un-gay" through legislation, many Christians simply want the government to regulate their homosexuality by relegating gays and lesbians into the back of society as though they would cease to exist.

For example, many pastors know that homosexuality is alive in their churches. But in order to maintain the appearance of normality, some pastors allow gays and lesbians to serve in ministry, just as long as they are not open with their homosexuality. Indeed, many churches have a "don't ask don't tell" policy of their own. In terms of the military, Don't Ask Don't Tell only served to perpetuate the appearance of normality. Pulling the carpet over the situation helped to maintain the façade.

The only logical thing Christians could hope to accomplish by opposing gay rights with legislation is to maintain an appearance and a façade. The problem with this is that we, as Christians, have no constitutional grounds to define what is traditional or normal for other citizens. Every individual is free to define what is normal and traditional for them. Likewise, we as Christians are free to define what is normal for ourselves, our families, and our churches.

This distinction should not cause Christians great concern. In actuality, this fact is a blessing in disguise for Christianity. Just as we cannot define what is normal for the broader society, society cannot define what is normal for us. Many of us have been so focused on keeping marriage rights away from gays and lesbians that we have not noticed the true conflict that looms on the horizon. As Christians, what will we do when societal norms label anyone who preaches and teaches that homosexuality is a sin as bigots? Indeed, this is the direction society is currently moving. If, and when, societal norms completely shift, we as Christians will be that much more grateful for the religious freedoms found in the Constitution. If we embrace and respect one another's constitutional freedoms now, the things we teach our families and preach in our churches will always be protected no matter how much those things may lie outside cultural norms. However, embracing the Constitution requires that we acknowledge the equal rights of all Americans. This is the true beauty of the Constitution: it protects and guarantees our personal rights, not by restricting the rights of those with whom we disagree, but by protecting their rights as well.

A Useful, Protracted Battle

The question of equal rights for gays and lesbians has served the Republican Party well for many years. The entire debate provides a never-ending stream of opposition from Christians and is yet another example of how our faith has been manipulated by fear: one that, consequentially, mobilizes our vote. Christians have routinely elected Republican politicians based on promises of returning America to traditional values. Yet, these politicians have done nothing to accomplish this goal beyond political rhetoric and symbolic gestures. The reason is that there is nothing they can do if those goals involve imposing on the rights of others. In this regard, the goal of keeping gays and lesbians from obtaining equal rights is a complete farce.

In the meantime, the Republican Party is making the best use of the debate. Just before every election cycle we see the party revving up the faithful Christian vote by stoking the fear of homosexuality. Also, notice, in every election cycle there is some type of initiative or proposition on the ballet that is aimed directly at driving Christians to the polls. Regardless of whether or not the proposition has any chance of passing, or whether it is constitutional, Republican strategists know that getting Evangelicals to the polls to vote on social-moral issues translates into votes for the Party.

Year after year and election cycle after election cycle, Christians have been agitated and mobilized based on issues that the Republican Party is incapable of changing. However, as long as they are able to draw out the debate and to delay the inevitable victory in the battle for marriage equality, the Republican Party will use the issue of homosexuality to win elections at the expense of progress. All the while, Republican leaders have been embracing several gay-rights groups in order to secure their votes as well. The GOP has been hedging its bet at the expense of our faith, our nation, and the rights of same-sex couples.

Every Christian and every American should be disgusted with the blatant willingness of the Republican Party use of Christian religious disapproval of homosexuality while simultaneously courting gay and lesbian groups for political gain. More than simply experiencing disgust, every Christian should refuse to be manipulated by political strategists, particularly on the issue of marriage equality. As difficult as this may be for many Christians, we must remember that God gives us the freedom to determine how we will live our lives. Likewise, our American political structure gives us the freedom to live by our own moral code. Restricting anyone's rights based on our personal, religious beliefs is as un-American as it is un-Christian.

5.

HEALTHCARE

> If anyone says, "I love God," and hates his brother, he is a liar; for he who does not love his brother whom he has seen cannot love God whom he has not seen. —1 John 4:20 (NIV)[99]

No issue in recent political history has fueled as much anger in our political discourse as the Patient Protection and Affordable Care Act: better known as Obamacare.[100] Cantankerous debate filled town hall meetings and political rallies across the nation. Protestors took to the streets en masse to oppose the legislation that was aimed at ensuring that all Americans had access to healthcare.

During the 2011 Republican Presidential Debate in Tampa, Florida, CNN moderator Wolf Blitzer posed a hypothetical question to Congressman Ron Paul. The question asked who would be responsible for taking care of a young man in his thirties who had not purchased a healthcare policy because he, like most in their youth, thought he would not need it. This hypothetical uninsured man later discovered that he would need extensive medical attention.[101] Unable to provide a direct answer because of how the question was posed, Congressman Paul addressed the issue of individual risks and responsibility.[102]

The moderator continued to press Congressman Paul on the same question, perhaps in an attempt to force an answer out of the congressman. He rephrased the question: "But congressman, are you saying that society should just let him die?"[103] Three voices, one after the other, shouted from the audience, "Yeah," while chuckles echoed through the room.[104] Congressman Paul then gave his answer, which was an adamant, no.[105]

THREE CHEERS FOR DEATH

What does this say about Americans that a segment would cheer for the death of individuals that have no healthcare? What does it say about a political party that purports to be the party of Christian values? Surely these examples can be rationalized away as anecdotal or anomalous. However, I believe it is indicative of modern politics. Anger, as a political tool, has relentlessly been used to get voters to the polls. Now this anger has manifested itself throughout our political discourse. Much more than a mere tool, anger has become a defining feature of the way in which we discuss politics.

HEALING AND HEALTHCARE

Why is the idea of the government ensuring that all citizens have access to healthcare repugnant to contemporary Republicans?[106] More pertinent to this discussion, why would we as Christians support a political party that uses anger and division to create opposition against providing every American with access to healthcare? God is obviously concerned with the health of His children:

> "Beloved, I wish above all things that thou mayest prosper and be in health, even as thy soul prospereth.—3 John 1:2 (KJV)

As Christians, we believe that God wants us all to be healthy. We believe this so much that we expect God to break the laws of physics and our known reality to provide us with a miraculous healing. Why, then, is it difficult for some of us to accept that God simply could use an effective healthcare system to keep us from getting preventable diseases in the first place? Some may answer this question with accusations of socialism and redistribution of wealth. Nevertheless, we have a responsibility as Christians to minister to the spiritually and physically hurting.

> We that are strong must bear the infirmities of the weak.—Romans 15:1 (KJV)

This Christian mandate was speaking explicitly about our individual faith. However, is it any less true if applied to our Christian responsibility to help the less fortunate in our society?

INSURANCE: REDISTRIBUTION AT WORK[107]

The irony of the debate over healthcare is that all types of insurance are forms of wealth redistribution. Redistribution collects the resources of citizens and distributes those resources to another segment. In other words, it pools the nation's resources in order to provide a benefit for either the entire nation, or a select few. Is this not the exact method insurance policies employ?

Everyone who enters into an insurance policy pools their money in order to spread the risks and to provide coverage for each other in the event someone gets sick, is involved in an accident or dies. Premiums from those of us who are relatively healthy are used to cover the treatment of those who are sick. Premiums from those of us blessed enough to have never gotten in an accident are used to pay for those that did. Dr. Donald Berwick, the former administrator for the Centers for Medicare & Medicaid Services, confirms this thought:

> "Those of us who have more because we are healthier...helps those of us who have less because we are not healthy."[108]

Those who staunchly oppose the Affordable Health Care Act based on the premise that it is redistribution miss the fact that insurance, by definition, is redistributive. The primary difference is that the profits of insurance companies are enjoyed privately by corporations while the benefit is provided through redistribution. Beyond the political explanation remains the Christian imperative: The Affordable Health Care Act, along with all types of insurances, gives us an opportunity to show compassion to our fellow man and, indeed, to ourselves when our time of medical need comes. Nevertheless, this particular debate has infuriated the nation on both sides of the debate.

One of the primary arguments against any type of redistribution is that it is equivalent to the government stealing from one group through taxation in order to provide for another group. Ironically, it was Christ himself that first taught us about a Christian's duty to pay taxes in the familiar story of the religious leaders attempting to entrap Jesus:

> Tell us, then, what you think. Is it lawful to pay taxes to Caesar, or not?" But Jesus, aware of their malice, said, "Why put me to the test, you hypocrites? Show me the coin for the tax" And they brought him a denarius. And Jesus said to them, "Whose likeness and inscription is this?" They said, "Caesar's." Then he said to them, "Therefore render to Caesar the things that are Caesar's, and to God the things that are God's."
>
> —Matthew 22:17-22 (KJV)

Healthcare

REDISTRIBUTING UP OR DOWN?

The reality of our political existence is that redistribution of wealth occurs every day. Our taxes are gathered and redistributed to whatever sector of the economy the government deems necessary. Whether the money goes to the troops in the military, defense contractors building new weapons, infrastructure upkeep, or social or corporate welfare, it is all redistribution of wealth. The real question at hand is whether or not the majority of Americans agree with where the redistributed funds go.

Many Americans bitterly opposed the "redistribution of wealth" through the new healthcare law which ostensibly redistributed from the rich to the poor. However, are these same Americans also opposed to the redistribution of wealth from the bottom to the top in the form of corporate welfare, subsidies, tax incentives, and tax breaks for the richest among us? This type of redistribution occurs every day. Billions of taxpayer dollars are spent annually on subsidies to help industries struggling to compete in the global market.

Our individual taxes will be paid. As Christians, Christ taught us to give to Caesar his tribute. The government actively redistributes our hard earned money to countless activities. While some of that redistribution goes to the poorest among us, some goes to the richest among us. If we are going to oppose redistribution, are we only going to oppose the wealth that is going down, or will we also oppose the wealth that is going up?

While the Republican Party created a frenzy of anger in America over Obamacare, the true tragedy of the debate finally dawned on me. So many Republicans and Evangelical Christians rallied in opposition to the idea of redistributing wealth to the poor through Obamacare. Although I was not poor, I realized that I would be one of the beneficiaries of Obamacare. I was in the middle-class. I had a full time job that allowed me to live an average American life; however, my job simply did not offer healthcare.

Ironically, other employees in our organization—who earned far less than I did—had access to healthcare. They were able to see a primary care physician and have regular checkups. They were able to do these things because the very poorest among us have Medicaid. While many middle-class Americans were shouting against Obamacare giving handouts to the poor, in actuality, they were rallying against their children's, neighbors', and their own interests. Obamacare addresses the gap that many hard working, middle-class families fall into.

Opposition against Healthcare or the President?

The true nature of politics is disturbing when you consider how the Republican Party so vehemently opposed the Affordable Care Act despite the fact that it was based on a Republican plan.[109] Anger towards a president has led them to turn their backs on policies that they once championed. The primary goal of the Republican Party, as stated by Senator Mitch McConnell, was to defeat President Obama.[110] They have opposed every single initiative set forth by the president in hopes of achieving this goal. Republicans went as far as opposing policies that they previously supported in order to oppose the President's agenda, which actually embraced those policies.[111] The Party maliciously opposes everything President Obama sets out to accomplish, determined to make him a one-term president. In that the Affordable Care Act was based on a Republican concept, if the GOP now holds that it is a socialist program, are they not conceding that they were the original authors of a socialist program? What's more, they only oppose it now because it is being offered up by the Democratic president. This political strategy has been extremely effective. Without question, this type of politics is not good for America. Unfortunately, this is the nature of modern politics.

Healthcare

This particular debate has sown so much discord among Americans, it is nearly impossible for citizens to discuss political topics without those debates devolving into bitter and angry arguments. Politically divisive issues have always been a part of our national discourse. However, the manner in which we opposed one another during the Healthcare debate introduced a new level of vitriol that our generation has never before seen. Perhaps the most tragic part of this debate is the amount of pure contempt and anger that has been generated because of it. Sadly, much of that anger has focused towards the poor. As Christians, whether we support or oppose the Affordable Care Act, we should be concerned with how much hatred is now being targeted on the very people Christ told us to care for: the least of these:

> For I was hungry and you gave food, I was thirsty and you gave me drink, I was a stranger and you welcomed me, I was naked and you clothed me, I was sick and you visited me, I was in prison and you came to me.' Then the righteous will answer him, saying, 'Lord, when did we [do all of these things]?' And the King will answer them, '...as you did it to one of the least of these my brother, you did it to me.'
> —Matthew 25:35-40 (ESV)

SHOULD CHARITY BE PRIVATE?

Republicans have stated that the Federal Government should not be involved in charity and that charity should be a private matter left up to individuals, charitable organizations, and churches. Indeed, there are phenomenal churches and programs across the nation that help families in their times of need. However, experience has taught me that it is unreasonable to look to the churches to fulfill the healthcare needs of the people.

GOD IS NOT A REPUBLICAN

Most pastors would agree that after church expenses and the upkeep are paid for, there is very little left to help the needy. Out of that small amount, churches do phenomenal things such as rent and utility assistance, food banks, and scholarships to parishioners and community members. Churches serve an invaluable role in the community. However, few churches, if any, are capable of fulfilling the healthcare needs of their congregants. No church is capable of filling the healthcare needs for those in the community that have no insurance.

I served in church for many years. The ministry did amazing things with the limited funds it had. However, the ministry was unable to provide health insurance to its employees. Without insurance, a five-hour visit to the emergency room cost me approximately $6000.[112] Multiply that estimate by the number of uninsured people in our nation. No amount of private charity, individual philanthropy, or church assistance could ever cover the amount needed for healthcare in our nation. Although the uninsured may be able to get emergency care, emergency room doctors do not treat cancer or other chronic illnesses. Only in the rarest of occasions can an uninsured individual get access to the type of healthcare needed to treat serious, chronic illnesses. Although the notion sounds noble, suggesting that churches and private charity are able to handle the needs of the uninsured in this country is wildly fatuous.

Anger as a Tool

It would seem as though anger politics is the most useful driver of political participation. This is evident by strategists making each election a referendum on the other party. Outrage over an issue drives people to the poles more than anything else. Outrage over the Affordable Health Care Act drove voters out to the mid-terms elections of 2010, and helped the Republican Party win a majority in the House of Representatives. That same wave elected Tea Party Governors across the nation.

What is, perhaps, the most ironic detail of anger politics is both parties' ability to cry foul when they are the victims of this tactic, simultaneously pretending as though they never use it. This is the delusional reality of modern day politics. Neither side is innocent yet both Republicans and Democrats attempt to cast themselves as the victim. How could either party claim to be moral, religious, or the party for Christian values, when it uses anger, hatred, and division in order to obtain political power.

Do American's need someone to be angry at, or is anger is the only emotion powerful enough to get us involved in politics? If either is the case, America's political future will be based on which party can make their base the angriest. We cannot blame anger peddlers for giving us the only thing powerful enough to move us to action. Regardless, what good could be in store for our nation if anger, hatred, and fear are all that drives our political participation?

The most disheartening reality is the manner in which many Americans adopt organized anger to be their own. This is not only true of Conservatives and Republicans; this is true for both sides of the debate. We allow professional operatives to give us the reasons for which we should be angry. We then adopt it into our psyche so deeply that it becomes extremely difficult to think objectively about the issues for ourselves. We internalize anger about things that we have, at best, only heard second hand.

Everything I do is Right.

Everything you do is Wrong.

Is there any hope for the future of our nation if politics causes us to believe that we are absolutely right and that our opposition is absolutely wrong? This is what contemporary American politics has been warped into. I often ask liberals and conservatives the same question: "Do you believe that everything would be better if we just got rid of all of the Liberals," or, "all of the Conservatives?"

The purpose behind this question is to help us think for ourselves about the implications. Do we sincerely want to get rid of anyone with whom we politically disagree? If anger has led us to believe that all we have to do is to silence our opposition, then our democracy is truly in trouble. What would America be without opposing ideas? What is freedom without dissenting voices? Without the voices of people with whom we disagree, America would no longer be free: it would no longer be America. It would be a single party nation flirting with authoritarian rule.

The Spiritual Question

It is not a question of whether Christ would be in favor of healthcare for all Americans. Trying to prove this is as futile as trying to prove that Christ was Republican or Democrat. But the spiritual question that arises from this entire debate is, "Why is so much anger focused on keeping healthcare from the poor?" This is no overstatement. The anger towards the poor is so great that it is palpable. Why?

Is it that we need to look down on someone in order to feel better about ourselves, or is it that we need to take our anger out on someone? Do we need to focus the latent anger about our individual plight in life onto someone else or to have someone to blame for it? Perhaps it is too difficult to be angry at ourselves, and so, instead of accepting where we are in life, we project that anger onto others, like the man who is, in fact, angry at his boss but takes it out on his family at home. Regardless, none of these traits is Christ like.

Politicians of all persuasions understand the power of anger. Strategists and operatives have mastered the art of refocusing anger and causing us to project it onto another group. Then we blame our struggles on the opposing voting bloc as though we were enemies. Sadly, many of us who indulged in these moments of refocused anger are Christians. Anger politics distracted us from our Christian responsibilities. This has been injurious to our personal witness and our collective faith. Furthermore, anger distracted us from what we were doing to ourselves. Where we thought we were keeping something from the poor, in actuality, we were keeping it from ourselves.[113]

Loosing Ourselves in Anger

Whatever you believe about the poor, we have a Christian duty not only to feed and clothe them, but also to love them. Charity in the spirit of bigotry is still bigotry. Anger causes us to lose ourselves and to forget our faith. It causes us to behave in a manner that Christ would never condone.

All of us are capable of acting out of character when we are filled with anger. In fact, it is safe to say that all of us have been guilty of it. This is the exact reason we must be so very careful not to allow professional rabble-rousers to give us the issue of the week for which we are to be angry. There is a time for righteous indignation; however, this moment is a personal and sacred one, not one to be ignited by political arsonists who sit back and watch as the flames become uncontrollable.

That is what Robert, an Ohioan suffering from Parkinson's disease, experienced as he sat in the street holding a sign explaining why he needed healthcare. Two opponents of the legislation took turns deriding him, with no sympathy for his condition. The first detractor stood on the corner of the street, talking down to Robert as though he were a child. The second taunted him by throwing dollars in his face. As he screamed in Robert's face, the second man derisively made it clear he, not the government, would decide when Robert would receive his charity and how much he would receive.[114]

Then there was the disabled woman from New Jersey's 6th Congressional District. She was stricken with several preexisting conditions that confined her to a wheelchair. She gave her testimony at a town hall meeting explaining why she needed Obamacare to pass in order for her to afford her treatments and medication. As she did, angry detractors heckled, jeered and interrupted every word, ultimately bringing her to tears.[115]

Then there was the mother whose son had just lost his wife and unborn child to double-pneumonia. The young couple had no insurance. The wife finally got treatment by telling the hospital she had coverage; however, it was already too late. As the heartbroken mother told of her family's loss, members of the audience laughed, booed, and heckled her also to the point of tears.[116]

All that these three individuals were seeking was an opportunity to let their story be heard. They wanted the chance to tell the world why they supported a bill aimed at giving every American access to affordable healthcare. Instead, what they found were men and women filled with so much anger and contempt that they would momentarily dismiss their faith and forgot to reciprocate the love that Christ had shown them. They weren't socialists advocating for the government to take from the rich in order to give to the poor. They weren't looking for handouts. All they were looking for was a chance to be heard. All they needed was healthcare.

6.

BLACK AND WHITE

EQUALLY CONSERVATIVE, EQUALLY DIVIDED

It is said that Sunday morning is the most segregated day of the week. It must also be said that Election Day is the most segregated day of the year. The greatest disconnect of conservatism is its inability to convert conservative, black Christians into conservative Republican votes.

Research shows that African-Americans are the most spiritually committed ethnic or racial group in the nation. Over half attend worship on a weekly basis. Three out of four pray on a daily basis. Nearly nine out of ten firmly believe that God exists. Approximately fifty-percent of African Americans think that homosexuality should be discouraged while over sixty-percent oppose gay marriage. The black community is divided on the issue of abortion with forty-one percent believing abortion should be illegal in most cases. What's more, African-Americans generally consider themselves to be conservative.[117]

There is much agreement between black Christian conservatives and white Evangelical conservatives. Yet, just as the White Christian Evangelical demographic overwhelmingly votes with the Republican Party, black Christian conservatives overwhelmingly vote with the Democratic Party.[118] As segregated as Christians are on Sunday morning, so too are their votes on Election Day. Although black pastors have stood alongside Republican politicians in opposition to gay marriage and

WHY BLACKS DO NOT VOTE REPUBLICAN

No racial or ethnic group is homogenous. The same is true for the African-American community. The political ideologies of African-Americans span the entire political spectrum from left to right; nevertheless, one thing can be said with certainty: blacks do not vote Republican—at least eighty-eight percent of them do not.[119]

While many African-Americans agree with Republicans on homosexuality and abortion, the majority of them still cannot bring themselves to vote for the Republican Party. Former Presidential candidate Herman Cain suggested that the reason blacks do not consider the Republican Party is because we have all been brainwashed.[120] The truth is, African-Americans actively vote in favor of whichever party they believe best serves their socio-economic and political interests.

After Abraham Lincoln and his Republican Party brought an end to slavery, African-Americans overwhelmingly supported that party.[121] At the time of the Civil Rights movement, the African-American vote was divided between the two major parties.[122] Blacks realized when their time with the Republican Party had come to an end. After the Democratic President, Lyndon Johnson, signed the Civil Rights Act into law, against the wishes of many in his party, the southern Dixiecrats defected to the Republican Party.[123]

Ninety-four percent of African-Americans voted with the Democratic Party in the election following the passage of the Civil Rights Act of 1964.[124] It is reasonable to conclude that blacks would once again move their voting bloc to another party if the time ever comes when the Democratic Party no longer serves their socio-economic and political interests.

Race Matters

It is worth mentioning the progression of my thought processes regarding race and politics. In my original version of this chapter, I intentionally attempted to play down the role of race in explaining why African Americans do not vote with the Republican Party. This was not because I believed race matters were irrelevant. However, in our modern political discourse, claims of racism and counter-claims of race baiting have obfuscated what otherwise would be a clear cut conversation. It is all but impossible to speak on matters of race without being labeled a racist or a race-baiter.

Most Americans, black and white, had hoped that America had truly become a post-racial society. Even with the uptick in white extremist activity after the election of President Obama, it still appeared that the national dialogue had moved into an era in which racism and race baiting were no longer acceptable.[125] To that end, I did not want race to become a distraction in this particular conversation on faith and politics. This was until the Republican Primaries of 2012.

The Southern Strategy

Former Speaker of the House, Newt Gingrich, openly and unashamedly revived what many describe as the Southern Strategy. This term was originally attributed to Richard Nixon's campaign strategy of using the terminology, "states' rights," to appeal to opponents of the civil rights legislation passed during the Johnson administration.[126] Many apply the term to Ronald Reagan and cite his masterful technique of stoking the latent racial sentiment of southern voters by using phrases such as "welfare queens" and "strapping young bucks" who were ostensibly taking advantage of food stamps and public housing.[127]

The technique was simple and painfully effective. Reagan was able to stir up the "Old South" while avoiding being labeled a racist himself. He never said, "black teenaged single moms" or "black sex-crazed men." He carefully chose phrases that did not allow his opponents to push back. It was so effective that even now as this book is being read, half of the readers will believe that I am race-baiting while others will consider the Southern Strategy as old news.

While most Americans, black and white, were striving to move beyond our jaded past, Newt Gingrich saw an opportunity to capitalize in the South. First, he suggested that poor kids have a low work-ethic because they come from neighborhoods in which they have no role models.[128] Notwithstanding the flaws in his logic, Gingrich could have been referring to poor kids of all ethnicities. Sadly, this was only the beginning.[129]

Next, Gingrich brought the insults closer to the black community by regarding Barack Obama as the "most successful food stamp president."[130] If the black community missed the first comment, they clearly heard the second one. Some commentators see Gingrich's statement as a matter of fact. More Americans are on food stamps today than ever before.[131] But for the black community, it was seen as a white man denigrating the first black president by attributing a welfare program that has historically been associated with our community despite the fact that blacks have never been the majority recipients of food stamps.[132]

Unfortunately for the nation, Gingrich was not finished. After insulting the first black president by calling him a "food-stamp president," Gingrich came full circle by saying that if the NAACP ever invited him to speak: "...I'll go to their convention to talk about why the African American community should demand pay checks and not be satisfied with food stamps..."[133]

This was the first time he addressed the black community directly with his carefully crafted words. To be fair, Newt Gingrich wasn't the only Republican candidate who was accused of racist rhetoric—just the most frequent. Former senator, Rick Santorum, said that he was "tongue tied" when he was recorded on video saying: "I don't want to make black people's lives better by giving them someone's money..."[134]

Although Speaker Gingrich was not alone in using the racially tinged rhetoric, it seemed as though the closer he got to the South Carolina Primary the more brazen he became. While most African-Americans were attempting to get their bearings after being blindsided by his previous display of racism, the politically astute saw through Gingrich's approach. The former Speaker was not a true racist. He was an opportunist. He understood what he needed to do in order to gain the advantage in the state that was first to secede from the Union. Gingrich knew what it would take and gave it all he had.[135]

THE SOUTH CAROLINA DEBATES

It was not until the South Carolina debates that Gingrich's approach came to a head. There was little surprise to Newt Gingrich's derisive response to Fox News® commentator, Juan Williams, question about his comments that were, "at a minimum offensive to all Americans, but particularly to blacks." The true surprise, however, was how openly the crowd booed Williams' nuanced question and cheered Gingrich's response.[136] Black Christian conservatives who watched on that evening—which, coincidently, was Dr. Martin Luther King Day—had to find it disturbing that an overwhelmingly white crowd would so enthusiastically boo what appeared to be the only black man in the room as he asked questions that were pertinent to their interests. The GOP did not get any closer to gaining minority votes that night.

Gingrich was so successful in employing the Southern Strategy that he received the first standing ovation in debate history and went on to win the primary by thirteen percentage points. This was an amazing comeback from being behind by twenty-five points just before the South Carolina debate. [137][138]

A great study for political scientists would be to research the political value of the Southern Strategy. For Newt, it gained him twenty-seven points in a single week. Although he won in South Carolina, the GOP lost ground in capturing the socially conservative African American vote. The progress in race matters that our nation has made over the decades lost ground because of his willingness to scratch a slowly healing scab, leaving behind a freshly opened wound.

Post-Debate Analysis

Perhaps minorities should not be so sensitive, taking offense to words that were not directly addressed to their community. However, consider if a black candidate alluded to the problem of crime in "trailer park" communities. Surely, there would be a portion of the white community that would instantly believe this candidate was talking about them. Regardless of how many minorities live in trailer parks, this group would be offended, and rightfully so.

Unfortunately, stereotypes remain. So when minorities hear a white man say things like, "blacks should ask for jobs and not welfare," or "the most successful welfare president ever," it should not be surprising that offense is taken, just as offense would be taken in the white community if a minority politician were to use derogatory stereotypes of white Americans.

While speaking at a town-hall meeting the day after his confrontation with Juan Williams, Gingrich was commended by an audience member. She applauded how Gingrich "put Juan Williams in his place."[139] To minorities this was insult to injury. Her words were indicative of the very concern that Williams attempted to express on behalf of blacks. Juan Williams was not a child that needed to be put in his place. He was an accomplished journalist who was asking a question that was important to an entire demographic group.

Her matter of fact tone not only harkened back to the days of racial segregation but also signified that a large segment of our society believed that anyone who *dared* to suggest that racism still exists needed to be "put in their place." Our

Black and White: Equally Conservative, Equally Divided

progress as a nation is delayed when counterclaims of race-baiting are used to discredit all claims of racism. Not every claim of racism is justified; however, this does not delegitimize every other claim.

The look in Gingrich's eyes as he listened to the woman's words was that of a man who realized he had opened Pandora's Box but had gone too far to turn back. Fastidiousness is an unspoken requisite for political office. You do not reach the level of Speaker of the House without understanding the value of carefully selecting every word. This is why it is reasonable to conclude that Speaker Gingrich knew exactly what he was saying and to whom he was saying it. He clearly felt that he could succeed in South Carolina by insulting minorities. Unfortunately, he was correct.

Race Baiting

As political commentator, Chris Matthews, stated in regards to this issue, "Either you hear the code being used, or you don't."[140] Either you read the previous paragraphs and labeled me a race baiter or you instantly understood what I was trying to convey. Nevertheless, the question at hand is, "why is it that so many conservative Christian blacks do not vote with the Republican Party?" Anyone with basic communication skills understands that perception is more important than what was said. What a listener heard is more important that what the speaker said.

If minorities feel as though racism still exists in the Republican Party, the Party will never receive the minority vote, regardless of agreement on social issues. There is the twelve percent of the black community who does not see or is not affected by the apparent, latent racism that of the Republican Party. There are the *Herman Cains* and the *Allen Wests* who openly reject the notion of racism in the Party.[141] But in this too, they are the minority.

GOD IS NOT A REPUBLICAN

Divergent Faith

Despite the relevance of race, it is an inadequate explanation of why conservative blacks Christians do not vote with conservative white Christians. Dr. Melissa Harris-Perry, Tulane University political science professor, addresses this conversation, not from matters of race but, rather, from matters of faith. According to Harris-Perry, African American Christians began to understand and interpret God from the vantage point first of slavery, then of segregation, and Jim Crow.[142] Black Christians had to grapple with being taught that God was a benevolent and loving creator while facing the realities of racism and segregation. How could God allow slavery and still be a benevolent God? How could God allow racism and be considered a loving God? This led to the infamous question, "Is God a white racist?"[143]

The struggle within black Christians to answer these troubling questions led African Americans to interpret God as a God of justice and liberation. As blacks looked at the reality of their plight in America, the only way they could accept the existence of a benevolent God was to understand him from the vantage point of the oppressed. Much like the Children of Israel suffering under the lash of Pharaoh, African Americans look to God to bring about freedom and, eventually, justice.[144]

This is the fundamental difference in how African Americans see God versus white evangelical Christians. It is safe to say, the reason white evangelicals had little need for a god to deliver them from oppression was because many of them were the oppressor during this period of time. While blacks were clinging to God for justice and deliverance, white evangelicals looked to God for other needs. African-American pastors preached for generations that God would one day deliver His people from oppression. Indeed, it was black preachers and their congregations that led the civil rights movement.

Nearly two generations removed from segregation, blacks still view God to be a liberator who will bring justice in an unjust society. This tradition in the African-American religious community runs as deeply as the blood in our veins. Even after the election of the first African-American president, many blacks still view God as the champion of the oppressed. Although the prosperity gospel represents a fundamental change in the core message of the black church, justice, equality, and liberation remains in the very DNA of the black Christian experience.

It is important to distinguish between matters of race and matters of justice. While very few Americans would suggest that racism is completely a thing of the past, most Americans would agree that America has made tremendous progress. To that end, African-Americans do not cling to the God of justice and liberation because of discrimination. Black Christians do not hold on to a liberation view of God because they have a need to be liberated from racism and slavery. Like Americans of all ethnicities, many African Americans feel the need to be liberated from economic oppression. This type of oppression transcends all races.

ECONOMIC JUSTICE

Every denomination of Christianity has sects that find it inconceivable that a Christian would vote for the Republican Party platform because of their economic policies. Catholics and Protestants both have large bodies of believers that view Republican economic policies as un-Christian because they believe those policies perpetuate economic exploitation, poverty, and greed.

I bring up these groups, not as an endorsement of their beliefs, but to contrast various schools of Christian political thought. Across the nation—indeed across the globe—there are Christians who vote just as fervently for political parties based on economic morality as American Evangelicals vote based on social morality. With eighty-eight percent of African-Americans voting with the Democratic Party despite the party's socially liberal positions, we can conclude that many black conservative Christians align with the school of Christianity that vote based on economic-morality issues.

The Prosperity Gospel

Harris-Perry's article revealed how the Republican Party could gain ground in the black community. Her research showed that black congregants that attended prosperity gospel based churches provide the Republican Party with its best opportunity for conversion.[145] Harris-Perry quantified what many black preachers have known for years: the prosperity gospel is fundamentally different from the theology of the traditional African American church:

> Two traditions of black ministry, Black Liberation Theology and the prosperity gospel have very different notions of Christ and therefore exert different influences on political action.[146]

The mega church phenomenon is still spreading across the nation. Many pastors are becoming more like life coaches, and less are taking the role as the prophet which speaks truth to power. Some of the largest churches in the nation are built on the theology of prosperity. Even without academic research, it is easy to see the differences between churches driven by the prosperity gospel and those that are rooted in the African-American tradition. Many modern African-American pastors are less like the ministers who led the Civil Rights movement and more like motivational speakers who use the Bible as their foundation.

This is not to say that the evolution of black preachers is necessarily bad thing for the black church. Many communities have been uplifted by mega churches and the prosperity gospel; however, it is clear that the focus of many African American preachers has shifted from biblically based equality and justice, to the prosperity gospel.

However, this shift represents a dynamic change in the core essence of what has driven black politics for generations. As more African-American Christians begin to perceive God from the vantage point of the prosperity gospel, less holds to the image of Christ as the God of justice and liberation. Dr. Harris-Perry explains that the Republican Party can gain the most ground in this shifting theological dynamic. This is because, the drivers of social justice and civil rights movements have been the churches built on liberation theology.[147]

SMALL AND BIG GOVERNMENT AND STATES RIGHTS

Allow me to offer another reason that the majority of blacks do not vote with the Republican Party despite their similar conservative social views, in addition to race matters, matters of economic justice, and perceptions of God. Research shows that many African Americans prefer a bigger government.[148] The Republican Party opposes big government and advocates for states' rights. This opposition consistent with the conservative belief that the bigger a government becomes the more likely it will infringe on the liberties of the individual. In this respect, many Republicans view state government as a haven from the federal government.

The number one argument of states' rights advocates in the Republican Party against the *Brown v. the Board of Education* decision of 1954 and the Civil Rights Act of 1964 was that both intruded on states' rights. Indeed, the federal government "delivered" blacks from segregation suffered at the hands of the states. If left up to the several states, it is possible that some school systems would still be segregated. Where Republicans look at the states as their refuge, African Americans have had to look to the federal government as theirs.

To conservatives who view the federal government as a threat to liberty, a politician can do no better than advocating that the government be so small that it can be drowned in a tub.[149] To minorities who have had to appeal to the federal government for their civil rights, services, and social justice, a federal government that small is more likely to leave us at the mercy of a state that is free to impose its sovereign will.

Similarities with Hispanic Voters

Republicans have a similar problem with Hispanic voters. Indeed, this chapter could have been about the religiosity of Latino voters as compared to the voting practices of Latino voters. Sixty two percent of Hispanic voters identify themselves as Catholic. Thirteen-percent of this demographic identifies as evangelical Christian.[150] The vast majority of Christian Hispanics prays daily, and believes that God is present and active in their daily lives.[151] Fifty-one percent of Hispanics believe abortion should be illegal in most cases.[152] In general, Hispanics are religiously conservative.

Although the contrast is not as stark as in the African American community, Hispanic Christians tend to favor the Democratic Party despite their conservative, religious views. Hispanic Catholics, despite opposition to abortion, vote forty-eight percent with the Democratic Party. This is compared to seventeen-percent who vote Republican.[153]

Considering the vast amount of anti-immigration rhetoric and the number of harsh policy changes across the country, these statistics should not come as a surprise. Hispanics, like African Americans, are making political decisions based on more than their faith. Perhaps, it is their interpretation of their faith that is informing their politics. Social justice has a firm footing in the Catholic Church. Nevertheless, one thing is evident. African Americans and Latino voters do not believe that God is Republican.

God is Not a Democrat

Political parties are incapable of completely satisfying the demands of each interest group gathered underneath its tent. Every group gives up something in order to be incorporated into the larger body. Democratic Christians give up some social issues in order to be aligned with a party they agree with on economic issues. Whether they are aware of it or not, many Republican Christians give up their economic interests in order to be aligned with a party that at least espouses their social beliefs.

To be certain, African-Americans take issue with the Democratic Party both for social and economic reasons. Indeed, many see the Republican and Democratic Parties as two sides of the same coin. Conservative black Christians take issue with the social platform of the Democratic Party as well as the timidity with which the party implements favorable economic policies. Nevertheless, many black Christians have been willing to push their concerns to the side and vote Democratic. Perhaps African-Americans are more satisfied with the slow, incremental change moving us in the direction of the Democratic Party than moving in the opposing direction of the Republican Party.

American politics requires for us to choose between what many believe to be "the lesser of two evils." The question all Americans are faced with is, "what issues are most important to me?" Those issues which we deem to be the most important determine which political party we support. Other issues become secondary. While many American Christians have lifted social-political issues as preeminent to God—and as such should be preeminent to us—there is clear biblical support for both sexual and economic morality. Other chapters have been dedicated to the question of whether the Republican Party has made any actual gains for social conservatives or not.

It should be clear, this majority of black conservative Christians have two very strong reasons for not giving the GOP their vote: the appearance of racism—justified or not—and irreconcilable differences on economic and social justice. A third, potential, reason is the affinity African Americans have towards the Federal Government; however, more research is needed to better substantiate this assertion. While some

Christians may not believe that economic morality matters to God, those who overwhelmingly find themselves on the bottom of the economic system are more likely to ask God for deliverance, not just from a sinful world, but from economic oppression.

•SECTION 2•
ECONOMIC MORALITY

About this Section

The following chapters deal with the robust topic of justice and the morality of Republican economic policies. Christian Evangelicals have been electing Republicans into office for over thirty years. The evangelical vote was cast in hopes of restoring traditional values to the nation. Although little has been done to advance the social agenda of Christians, much has been done to advance the conservative economic platform.

Our votes have not brought about social morality: they have brought economic immorality. Today, many Christians are either oblivious or indifferent to the effects a generation of supply-side economics has had on the poor, the middle class, and the nation as a whole. This section addresses the immoral nature of the Republican Party's economic policies over the last generation which can be simplified as follows:[154]

1. The government should encourage economic growth by cutting taxes.
2. Taxes should not be raised under any circumstances.
3. The government should not interfere with the markets because they are able to regulate and correct themselves.[155]
4. The value of investments is greater than the value of labor; therefore, investments should be protected and taxed at a lower rate.[156]
5. Redistribution of wealth to the poor in the form of social safety-nets is un-American, hurts businesses, and robs the individual of their most basic driver for working: survival. "If a man does not work, he does not eat."[157]
6. The government should not be involved with forcing charity (through taxation). Charity should be a private decision.

Each of these six points is derived from Classical Economic theory. Each is an endorsement of laissez-faire capitalism. Therefore, this section is an earnest conversation on the positive and negative effects capitalism has on our society. We engage this conversation in the context of the interplay be-

About this Section

tween economic morality, justice, and the tenets of Republican economic policy.

The tone of this section is uniquely different from the other portions of this book. It is more academic, theological and theoretical. However, this section is critical in understanding how the Christian vote has not been used to pass moral legislation but, rather, to change tax policy and to enact economic policies that are contrary to Christian values.

7.

THE GOD OF JUSTICE

Indeed, I tremble for my country when I reflect that God is just; that His justice cannot sleep forever." -Thomas Jefferson[158]

What is justice? If you were to ask fifty citizens, you would likely get fifty different answers. For some, justice is interpreted to mean *fairness* and *equity*. For others, justice is the rule of law, respect for private property, and the enforcement of contracts. For another segment, justice is a combination of all of these principles. In many respects, justice—much like beauty—is in the eye of the beholder.

DEFINING SOCIAL JUSTICE

It is when we use the term, social justice, that we see the clearest differences in opinion, definition, and interpretation. Although the definition of justice may be ambiguous, it is vitally important that it is clearly defined here. The Catholic Church's catechism on Social Justice provides will serve as the authority for this discussion:

> Society ensures social justice by providing the conditions that allow associations and individuals to obtain their due. The equality of men concerns their dignity as persons and the rights that flow from it...The equal dignity of human persons requires the effort to reduce...social and economic inequalities. It gives urgency to the elimination of sinful inequalities.[159]

Based on this Catholic catechism—which is steeped in biblical doctrine and centuries of theology—we can derive a Christian principle that actively seeks equal rights for all mankind and the reduction of "excessive social and economic inequalities."

What Social Justice is Not

There has been a concerted effort on the part of political conservatives, along with some Christians, to imbue a nefarious connotation onto the term "social justice." This is why definitions are extremely important. Some opponents of social justice would like to define it as being equivalent to socialism. The most prevalent definition of socialism in the American psyche is simply "bad" or "evil." And while the average American may be unable to define socialism accurately, they would at least tell you that it is something bad for our country.

Opponents of social justice benefit from this oversimplification. They seek to imply that social justice means the government would redistribute the nation's wealth so that all citizens own the same exact share. This is economic definition of socialism: one taken to the fullest extreme of the economic theory. This is not the biblical definition of social justice, nor is it the definition to which most advocates adhere. Social justice is not socialism.

The Watering Down Biblical Justice

Equating social justice with socialism has given many Christians the excuse to ignore or redefine our biblical call to seek equal rights for all citizens. It also causes many believers to avoid any policies that would reduce the "excessive" inequities in our political and economic systems. The neutralization of our Christian imperative for social justice because of our fear of socialism is not by mistake. Although the Catholic Church's definition of social justice does not call for pure socialism or communism, it is still a threat to conservative social and economic policies.

> The equal dignity of human persons requires the effort to reduce excessive social and economic inequalities. It gives urgency to the elimination of sinful inequalities.[160]

Seeking to reduce "excessive" inequalities first requires an admission that there are inherent inequalities in our political and economic systems. It is most unfortunate that some in the modern Republican Party would have us to believe that people are in poverty because they do not work hard enough.[161] More disturbing than this is assertion is the illogical and unbiblical teaching that poverty is the result of a mindset. The Book of Isaiah states:

> Woe to those who make unjust laws, to those who issue oppressive decrees, to deprive the poor of their rights and withhold justice from the oppressed of my people, making widows their prey and robbing the fatherless."
> —Isaiah 10:1-2 (NIV)

This scripture identifies the reality that injustices are often embedded in our system, which requires a systemic solution. Working poverty is a reality in our nation. It is disingenuous and insulting for anyone, including Republicans—and especially Christian Republicans—to perpetuate the notion that poverty is the result of slothfulness or a mindset. Poverty is real.

The Republican Party also supports the idea that poverty is the result of immorality. They cite the number of children born into single-parent homes and out of wedlock as one of the driving factors in poverty.[162] While this may be a contributing factor, it is in no way the only factor. This is a Straw Man argument created to divert attention away from the institutionalized causes of poverty. It is also used to endorse government intervention in morality. The fallacy is quite simple. Suggesting that morality is the cause of poverty also suggests that all one needs to do to get out of poverty is "behave themselves." This is both ridiculous and insulting to families and individuals who are both moral, hardworking, and yet remain in poverty.

There are those in our society who do not want an honest day's pay for an honest day's work. This phenomenon stretches the full range of our social strata. From the wealthy to the impoverished, there are those who work extremely hard and those who hardly work at all. If hard work was all that was needed to be successful, surely those living in poverty would be wealthy when we take into account the countless hours they work at jobs many of us would never consider. In reality, it is often the lowest paid employees on a job that have the hardest type of labor. Everyone that is rich did not necessarily get there as a result of persistent and hard work. Everyone living in poverty did not get there because they were lazy.

Private Charity or Governmental Resources?

Republicans suggest that charity should not be a function of the government and should be left to non-profits and churches. This is erroneous for two reasons: (1) Charity can only assist and temporarily take care of the poor. Charity is not a means of addressing inequalities that Christians are called to address; (2) Inequities that perpetuate injustices and poverty are embedded in our system; therefore, they require systemic remedies. Churches cannot fix unjust laws. Policy makers in the government can. Churches are not in the position to fix institutionalized poverty. However, policy makers in the government are.

Modern Republican politicians verbally advocate for a purely laissez-faire economy with no interference from the government for any reason. However, in practice they seek favorable conditions for corporations and the wealthy—or the so called "job creators." These policies are not necessarily a bad thing. The more attractive our nation is to corporations the more likely they will remain in the US.

However, the problem arises when we are faced with the decision between continuing corporate welfare at the expense of social welfare or even the general welfare.[163] When the government resources are so limited that it requires competition—which is almost always the case—the church should be leading the way in advocating for resources targeted at social justice.

There is no Christian imperative for us to advocate for businesses and the wealthy. They are not the enemy. They are not evil. Indeed, many of us aspire to own a business and to be wealthy. However, it is the Church's job to seek an end to the inequalities of our system that keeps many citizens from ever getting the opportunity to move ahead. The only way to accomplish this is through government action and resources. This means that the Church will, from time to time, find itself on the opposing side of advocates for corporations and the wealthy.

CHRISTIAN CONFLICT WITH THE REPUBLICAN PARTY

One of the most fundamental pillars of the Republican Party platform is advocacy on behalf of the business community or the wealthy. Long before social conservatives entered the coalition in 1980, the establishment included wealthy business owners. Evangelical Christians began voting with the Republican Party once the Party realized they needed to include social conservatives in their coalition. By adopting traditional values and the anti-abortion movements, the Republican Party was able to solidify the Evangelical Christian vote. Although it seemed as though this was the perfect coalition, the Christian imperative for social justice has always been at odds with Republican economic policies.

This is why it has been necessary for many in the Party to shift the term, social justice, from its true biblical definition and equate it to socialism—with all of the negative connotations that this term implies. By doing this, the Republican Party is able to keep Evangelical voters focused on their duty to social morality and not on economic morality. What is worse, there is a concerted effort to water down the Christian definition of social justice so that it would no longer pose a threat to the Republican Party. Now, many of these Christians can look at the world and manage to see immorality of thousands of children being aborted every day but take little notice of the institutionalized reasons behind the thousands of young children that die globally from hunger *every day*.

Christianity, in its totality, considers both the number of that die from abortion as well as the number of impoverished children that die from malnourishment. Christianity seeks social morality as well as economic morality. The Bible clearly addresses matters of justice, equality, and deliverance from oppression—both spiritual and economic. Nevertheless, many Christians are now divided on the issues and the appropriate means of remedying them. This is not because one side is right and the other is wrong. It is not because some want only to support spiritual morality with no regard for social justice and economic morality. It is because, for many years, the American political system has forced Christians to choose sides, neither of which is capable of living up to the totality of the Christianity.

Thomas Jefferson was justified in his concern for the nation. God is a God of justice. Isaiah prophecies that God's justice will not sleep forever:

> Our courts oppose the righteous, and justice is nowhere to be found. Truth stumbles in the streets, and honesty has been outlawed. Yes, truth is gone, and anyone who renounces evil is attacked. The LORD looked and was displeased

to find there was no justice. He was amazed to see that no one intervened to help the oppressed. So he *himself* stepped in to save them with his strong arm, and his justice sustained him.—Isaiah 59:14 (NLT)

If we as Christians do not fulfill our duty to justice, indeed, God will.

8.

KINGDOM OF GOD ECONOMICS

There are many articles and sermons that suggest that the Bible supports or endorses capitalism. Biblical capitalism in America came in response to the thriving social gospel of the early twentieth century which emphasized the duty of man to one another. A concerted campaign to use Protestant churches began as a means of opposing communism and supporting capitalism. Most notably during the Cold War, Billy Graham preached of the biblical principles of private property and individualism. Those words became a ringing endorsement for biblical capitalism.[164]

The debate over the relationship between biblical principles and various economic systems has been ongoing for centuries. While there are scriptures that seem to endorse capitalism, one cannot assert with theological integrity that the Bible supports any man-made economic model. This is not a modern debate. In his 1944 classic, The Condition of Man, Lewis Mumford noted:

> Protestantism in religion came into being, not as an ally of capitalism, but as its chief enemy: not as an effort to swell the energies of the id[165] but to curb them before they had become too powerful ...Protestantism was an attempt to check the commercial spirit and prevent it from getting hold of the Church.[166]

Mumford references fifteenth and sixteenth century theologians to support his claims.[167] There were great debates during this period over which system was the true Christian economic system. For some, it meant capitalism. For a large dissenting group of Protestants, it meant, in Mumford's words, "Christian Communism." Different interpretations have persisted for centuries. While many young and idealistic theologians, fundamentalists, and activists attempt to link the Bible with capitalism, they must consider several key biblical principles that conflict with capitalism.

THE YEAR OF JUBILEE

> And you shall consecrate the fiftieth year, and proclaim liberty throughout the land to all its inhabitants. It shall be a Jubilee for you; and each of you shall return to his possession, and each of you shall return to his family. ...Therefore you shall not oppress one another, but you shall fear your God; for I am the Lord your God. ...The land shall not be sold permanently, for the land is Mine; for you are strangers and sojourners with Me.
> —Leviticus 25:10, 17, 23 (NKJV)

The biblical economic system first establishes that all land and property belong to God. The Year of Jubilee was established so that the original allocation of property divided among the twelve tribes of Israel would always be intact. No matter how the land changed hands it would always be restored to the family it was first distributed to.[168] This was the Year of Jubilee.

The purpose of Jubilee, according to Leviticus, was to ensure that the Israelites did not oppress one another. This scripture acknowledges two important factors about human economics. First, it recognizes that mankind has a natural propensity to oppress one another through economic activity. Second, the scripture recognizes that oppression can occur naturally through normal economic exchange. Bad business decisions can lead to the oppression of an entire family.

Kingdom of God Economics

The Year of Jubilee ensured that no matter how poorly a family's land was managed, the family would always be restored with their original property after fifty years. Jubilee is in many ways the truest biblical example of redistribution. Jubilee also represented the year in which all debts were forgiven and slaves were freed. Many interpret Jubilee to be the year in which all citizens were given a clean slate.[169]

Usury and Interest

Perhaps the number one biblical principle that conflicts with the American economic system is the dependence of our system on charging interest. Without interest, capitalism does not work. This not only applies to financial capitalism—which solely depends on charging interest to generate profits—but also manufacturing—which depends on loans from banks to purchase equipment and property. Interest is the backbone of our economic system, yet the Bible clearly states that we should not charge usury in multiple scriptures:

> If you lend money to any of My people who are poor among you, you shall not be like a money-lender to him; you shall not charge him interest.
> —Exodus 22:25-27 (NKJV)

> In you they take bribes to shed blood; you take usury and increase; you have made profit from your neighbors by extortion, and have forgotten Me,' says the Lord GOD.—Ezekiel 22:12, (NKJV)[170]

> You shall not charge interest to your brother -- interest on money or food or anything that is lent out at interest. To a foreigner you may charge interest, but to your brother you shall not charge interest, that the LORD your God may bless you in all to which you set your hand in the land which you are entering to possess. — Deuteronomy 23:19-20 (NKJV)[171]

Without the ability to charge interest on money loaned to others, the entire financial system would never have existed. Based on this mere fact alone, it becomes impossible to claim that the Bible supports Capitalism. In no way should this be interpreted as suggesting that Christians advocate for the end of capitalism. It simply means that we cannot theologically support it, or any other economic system, with sound doctrine.

Public Charity in the Bible

While most Christians believe in charity and caring for the poor, many Republican Christians oppose government programs aimed at poverty relief. In general, Republicans advocate for private charity and not the "forced redistribution of wealth" through tax policy. There is, however, a biblical basis for poverty relief that is administrated publicly:

> At the end of every third year you shall bring out the tithe of your produce of that year and store it up within your gates. And the Levite...and the stranger...and the fatherless and the widow who are within your gates, may come and eat and be satisfied, that the Lord God may bless you in all the work of your hand which you do.
> —Deuteronomy 14:28-29

One of the best treatments of this scripture comes from a book entitled, *What the Bible Says about Everything*:

> To help these groups, the Law said that a tithe (or ten percent_ of every third years' produce should be set aside for their use. It was to be stored 'within your gates,' indicating that the aid should be collected and administered by towns and cities, not by individual households...The regularity of the third-year tithe...made this a systematic, not a haphazard, program of relief.[172]

Kingdom of God Economics

If this principle were applied to our current economic system, it would be equivalent to the government redistributing ten percent of the profits of every business and every individual to the poor. This is unimaginable in our current political reality.

PRIVATE CHARITY IN THE BIBLE

Private citizens had a responsibility to charity, in addition to the public programs.

> And when you reap the harvest of your land, you shall not reap your field right up to its edge, nor shall you gather the gleanings after your harvest. You shall leave them for the poor and for the sojourner: I am the Lord your God.
> —Leviticus 22:23 (NIV)

Several principles leap from this text. The first is the private responsibility to allow the poor to glean from the harvest. Glean means to gather or collect. If we apply this principle to today's society, God is instructing us to give portions of our goods, products, and profits to the poor. This is both radical and unimaginable. If a poor person came to an individual or a business and asked to glean from their profits, it would not matter that their request was a biblical principle. That person would undoubtedly be escorted off the property by security.

The second principle, and most important, is the continued usage of the phrase, "I am the Lord your God." If read in context, it becomes evident that God felt it necessary to remind us that He, not our wealth, is our god. By privately sacrificing portions of our wealth, honoring the Year of Jubilee, and participating in the publically administered poverty relief programs, the Israelite demonstrated that his commitment was more to God than it was to his wealth.

Whenever we give to the poor, the most important principle for us to understand is that our giving is not about the poor; it is about our willingness to sacrifice our wealth to demonstrate that our wealth does not control us. Unfortunately, when most of us think of charity we think that we are helping the poor person. In this scripture, God lets us know that we are, in actuality, helping ourselves not become a slave to our wealth.

MAN'S INABILITY TO INTERPRET

Indeed, it is possible to extrapolate scriptures and infer some capitalist principles.[173] Likewise, we can also extrapolate scriptures and infer socialist or even communist economic principles.[174] Furthermore, the Bible can be—and has been—used to justify and endorse slavery.[175] If Christians use the Bible to endorse capitalism, what is to be done with the scriptures that endorse slavery, socialism, or communism? At best, interpreting the Bible in a manner which exhorts one economic system above another is "reading into the text" or "making the text say something it does not explicitly say." This is known as eisegetical interpretations.[176] Theologians frown upon this technique because it can be misleading or intentionally deceptive. Christian author and blogger, Efrem Smith, said it best:

> [T]here are parts of the value system of God's Kingdom that sound socialist on first listen and there are parts on first listen that sound like empire [capitalism] But, when you look at all that is the Kingdom of God now and into eternity it is so much more than any earthly government could ever accomplish.[177]

Smith's words paralleled those of Dr. Martin Luther King Jr. in his sermon on Communism:

As Christians, we should not use the Bible to justify any

> We must honestly recognize that truth is not to be found either in traditional capitalism or Marxism. Each represents a partial truth. ...The Kingdom of God is neither the thesis of [Capitalism] nor the antithesis of [Collectivism], but a synthesis which reconciles the truth of both.[178]

particular political-economic structure. This is not the mandate we were given by Christ. What is more, doing so suggests that we understand God enough to be able to implement the economic system of the Kingdom of God. No theologian, preacher, or prophet can claim to know God enough to institute His economic system. Without question, mankind is incapable of interpreting and implementing the true economic system of the Kingdom of God.

9.

MORALITY OF CAPITALISM AND THE FREE MARKETS

There are nearly as many definitions for capitalism as there are for justice. As before, it is imperative that we clearly define our usage of the word. Our usage of the word through this section is best defined by the Oxford® Dictionary of Philosophy:

> Capitalism [is the] mode of socioeconomic organization in which a class of entrepreneurs and entrepreneurial institutions provide the capital with which businesses produce goods and services and employ workers. In return the capitalist extracts profits from the goods created."[179]

It is, once again, important to determine what we *do not* mean when we say "capitalism." When we use the term throughout the book we do not mean democracy. Many people mistake capitalism to mean democracy. Indeed, a nation can have a capitalist economy and a communist political system. The best example of this is China. Finally, we do not use the term to mean "free market." Free-market means the economic forces of supply and demand determine the outcome of a product or even a business. There has yet to exist a true free-market.[180] What presently exists are economies with varying degrees of influence over the market-place—both governmental influence as well as the powerful influence of private interests. Although U.S. markets may have much less influence asserted over it than other nations, it still has influences and interference.

The previous chapter alluded to the forces that institutionalize poverty and create systemic injustices. This requires a discussion on capitalism. If we as Christians are ever to be able to address the "excessive" inequalities that are inherent to our economic system, we must understand several underlying principles of the system.

Capitalism in America

In many ways, American capitalism is played as a zero-sum game.[181] This only means that there will be winners and losers. Capitalism, in the most simplistic sense, is about gathering wealth by producing goods and services people want to consume. The more that is consumed the wealthier the producers become. The structure of capitalism often requires producers to hire the cheapest labor possible in hopes of increasing productivity and profitability. Producers seek to charge the consumer the highest prices possible without impacting demand for their product.

The reality of American capitalism is that there is less manufacturing and more financing of debt. We are now in an era where wealth is generated by capitalists producing debt instruments to sell to the consumer. The more debt we consume, the wealthier the producers become and the more impoverished the consumers of debt become.

These principles are not an indictment of capitalism; they are merely some of the forces that contribute to institutionalized poverty. To that end, every good capitalist must scour the global market in order to find the cheapest labor possible to create their products and sell it at the maximum price possible.[182] The investor has an incentive to see the price of his investment increase. We see this in the prices of commodities. The most obvious example that each of us can identify with is the price of gas. High oil prices benefit oil investors at the expense of oil consumers.

The Result: Winners and Losers

Millions of Americans have lost their jobs to overseas outsourcing. Businesses have a profit incentive to keep employees' wages at the lowest level possible without stifling the workers' productivity. More Americans are in debt today than at any other time in the nation's history. The prices of commodities continue to increase, burdening the consumer while speculators profit. This reality does not make capitalists, corporations, or banks evil; they are simply working within the framework of the American economic system.

Every decision that is good for business is not necessarily a good decision for their employees or for the American people. Nevertheless, many of us have accepted the idea that businesses can do no wrong: as long as they continue to help grow the economy.

The Inherent Vice of Capitalism[183]

> For the love of money is a root of all kinds of evils. It is through this craving that some have wandered away from the faith and pierced themselves with many pangs.
> —1 Timothy 6:10 (ESV)

Capitalism is a tool. It is an amoral economic system that, by itself, is neither good nor evil. The method in which the capitalistic system is used determines the morality of it. An innovator who builds a company from the ground up in order to bring a vision to life then shares that vision with the world represents the best of capitalism. Many of these innovations are the very discoveries that have enriched millions of lives. No one should be envious of the vast wealth acquired by these types of capitalists. These capitalists represent the best of the American dream and, indeed, what many of us aspire to.

There is another type of capitalist to consider. This type can be categorized as individuals who seek their fortune by creating new forms of debt, by ravaging viable companies in order to make a profit, or by engaging in unethical practices for the sake of profit. This distinction is not an imaginary one based on any type of disdain for our economic system. It is a grim reality that can be seen in the weekly. There is a major difference between these two types of capitalists. Both groups are given the hollowed title of "job creators" and "innovators." While both may be out to make a living or to make a fortune, there is a fundamental difference in the true nature of what drives them: greed versus self-interest. As Adam Smith aptly noted in his seminal work, *An Inquiry into the Nature and Causes of the Wealth of Nations*:

> It is not from the benevolence of the butcher, the brewer, or the baker that we expect our dinner, but from their regard to their own interest.[184]

Smith titled this self-interested driver of economic activity as the Invisible Hand.[186] From this concept, we understand that the goods that we purchase, which add value to our daily lives, come as the result of someone else seeking their own interest, not from their benevolence or concern for humanity. Indeed, self-interest is a powerful driver of innovation and progress. It is not always someone with the best of intentions who changes the world for the better. Often, the ones who change the world were simply looking to change their personal economy—to make millions for self.

> I have never known much good done by those who affected to trade for the public good.
> —Adam Smith[185]

There are those who disdain capitalism because of the self-interested driving mechanism. In many respects, it strips any moral sentiment away from economic activities. It is when there is a deficiency of morality in our actions that we see things such as Enron, Mortgage Default Swaps, and the "Kids for Cash" judicial scandal in Pennsylvania.[187] Many advocates of capitalism quote Adam Smith as a justification of "the ends justifying the means."

However, Smith was not the economic Machiavellian some believe him to be. He had a deep sense of economic morality. Smith maintained a belief that was built on Immanuel Kant's philosophy that the moral quality of an action should only be determined by the intentions of the person.[188] So when Smith suggested that we not look to businessmen and women to make society better by their actions, he did not give them a pass from moral obligation in all of their actions. Although Adam Smith did not believe capitalists had to be benevolent, he did not excuse them to do evil.

Profit by Any Means?

This now highlights the fundamental problem with our economic system: human nature. There is no moral problem with capitalism. There is a moral problem with a society which allows—as well as endorses—the pursuit of money by any means deemed necessary. It is not the pursuit of money that is evil or detrimental to society. Injustices do not occur simply because of an individual's pursuit of profit. Injustices occur when profit is pursued with no regard to the methods. Injustices occur when we allow "greed" to be synonymous with "self-interest."

There are many behaviors that are legal but unethical. There are many business practices that, although legal, should make moral citizens—especially Christians—cringe. Our basic humanity should not allow us to turn a blind eye to inherently immoral activities simply because they are done in the name of capitalism, free markets, or profits. Without question, Christians should have the loudest voices which decry unethical behavior. As Christians, we should never allow ourselves to accept behavior that is driven by greed or has no regard for the fellow man.

While some social justice oriented Christians and non-religious activists look at capitalism with disdain, they have placed the target on the wrong culprit. It is not the economic system that is the problem. Problems arise when citizens pursue profit with no regard for the effects that pursuit has.

An even greater problem exists with some free market activists—many of which are from the Republican Party—are attempting to remove any government constraints that would potentially regulate this type of behavior. While it is not the responsibility of business-people to be benevolent, they should not, have the freedom to operate unethically in the name of profit-making.

Unregulated Capitalism

Capitalism is much like a room full of toys in which we are all children. Unregulated capitalism is what that room would look like without adult supervision. The most aggressive and greediest children fight all others to get the most toys possible. Without the presence of an adult or the presence of their teachings and admonitions, the child with the most greed, forcefulness, or size, wins.

Unregulated capitalism allows greed to be the only driver of our economic system. The world has already seen what this looks like. Not only, does it look like the Bernie Madoffs and the Scott Rothsteins[189] of the world, it also looks like our American past in which slaves and children were used for cheap labor and women were paid less simply because they were women.

Not only in our past, but presently are we able to see the results of unregulated capitalism. Banks turn overdraft fees into a billion dollar business by rearranging purchases to maximize fees, only to pay a few million in order to settle class action lawsuits.[190] Employees work for thirty years trusting their savings and pensions to the stock market, only to see their life savings disappear while investors who bet against the market collected millions. Without the appropriate amount of regulation, the government leaves the unscrupulous children in a room full of toys with no adult supervision.

This analogy can be more accurate by introducing teenagers—corporations and banks—into the room. These teenagers have been around for many more years than the younger children. They have mastered the art of getting the smaller kids to willingly give up some of their toys while forcefully taking the toys others.[191] By the time the younger children realize the dynamics of the game, they discover that they are completely at the mercy of the teenagers. Capitalism needs adults in the room in order for it not to implode:

> If men were angels, no government would be necessary. If angels were to govern men, neither external nor internal controls on government would be necessary.—James Madison[192]

Free Market Utopianism

The new move in the Republican Party is, in many respects, the most extreme interpretation of Adam Smith's Invisible Hand. Many in the GOP firmly believe and advocate for a completely free market system. This would mean that our economic system would operate without any government intervention or regulation. The rational for this belief is the premise that the free market is capable of regulating itself. For example, some believe there is no need for bureaucracies such as the Food and Drug Administration. It is their contention that the free market would push out any company that produced medication—or any other product for that matter—that was harmful. Once consumers become aware of the danger, demand for the drug would dissipate and the firm that produced the bad product would be replaced by competition.

Great irony lies in the fact that the Republican Party labels anyone who dreams of how our economic system could be better as "Utopians." Their dreams of a free market are indeed utopian. The free market has never truly existed in American history.[193] There has always been both government intervention as well as undue influence from powerful corporations and wealthy individuals. Each of these factors interferes with a truly free market.

The Gilded Age represented a period of time in which laissez-faire economics—free markets—prevailed. Admirers of this period see the tremendous economic growth and the vast accumulation of wealth by icons such as John D. Rockefeller, Cornelius Vanderbilt, and Andrew Carnegie. Others look to the effects businesses had on society as a whole. A handful of Americans created unimaginable wealth. Some accomplished this through the exploitation of citizens, and corrupt business practices and political behavior.

During this period, there was little regard to the consequences the actions of the wealthy had on society. The most extreme example of this is the advent of Social Darwinism. This philosophy expanded on the theory of Evolution and Natural Selection, equating it with the economic survival of the fittest. It advocated for the survival of the economic fittest. In 1883—at the height of the Gilded Age—Yale University professor, William Graham Sumner wrote:

> A pauper is a person who cannot earn his living...who cannot...pay his way. "...A man who does not contribute either by land, labor, or capital to the work of society, is a burden." On

> no sound political theory ought such a person to share in the political power of the State. He drops out of the ranks of workers and producers. ...he must be cancelled from the ranks of the rulers likewise.[194]

Sumner believed that a person who was impoverished or unemployed should not have the right to vote. It was not enough simply to consider them a burden on society: he believed their lack of ownership and productivity should disqualify them from participating in the society. Sadly, there are some politicians who believe this today.[195]

This period in history represents the closest America ever was to a free market. It was a period in which the wealthy considered the poor as burdens needing to be cast off. While it was a period of great growth and wealth accumulation, it was also a period in which the end justified the means. Wealth at any cost was the moral standard of the day.

Ironically, even during the period in American history in which there was no obligation to economic morality, free market capitalism still did not exist. Yet, modern Republican proponents of this theory insist that the solutions to our nation's woes lie in this utopian system. Advocates believe the answer is a smaller government with few, if any, regulations along with the rule of the free market. Seldom do they ever mention the effects that this dystopia would have on society as a whole because of their fixation the wealth potential. Indeed, it is a utopian fantasy.

Lack of Vision

Since this discussion is dealing with utopias, allow me to forward one of my own that is based both on the constitutional and biblical concept that all men are created equal. This idea is also based on Adam Smith's assertion that every child has the same potential as any other child:

> The difference of natural talents in different men, is...much less than we are aware of. The difference...seems to arise not so much from nature, as from habit, custom, and education. When they came in to the world, and for the first six or eight years of their existence, they were, perhaps, very much alike...About that age...they come to be employed in very different occupations. [196]

This passage, from Adam Smith, reflects his belief that every child is born with a similar capacity for achievement. The difference that we see in the "philosopher" and the "porter" is the result of upbringing, education, and opportunity. Regardless of where life takes an individual, each has the same human potential for greatness.

Imagine a world in which we looked at every individual as an asset to society. Every person would be viewed as someone with unique potential that, if ever realized, would be beneficial to society as a whole. In this world, a person would be looked upon in regards to what they could contribute to society. Instead of seeing individuals as tools from which we can extract wealth in order to make a few wealthy, we would see them as someone we could pull greatness out of—in order to make society as a whole more wealthy.

What if we looked at every individual as a potential Steve Jobs, Mother Theresa, Adam Smith, or Benjamin Franklin? It would not matter whether their contribution to society was a great sonata, the cure for a dreaded disease, or a business that employed thousands of citizens. All that would matter would be that every citizen had an opportunity to achieve their individual greatness to the benefit of the entire society. The primary challenge in life would be for them to discover and realize their potential. There would need to be an education system focused on developing unique individuals rather than carbon copies groomed in methods of the Industrial Revolution. Capitalism would continue to be the engine generates wealth from these unique gifts. Instead of depending on a small few, this utopia would see the greatness of all 300 million minds.

For hundreds of years, we have allowed capitalism to be played as a zero-sum game in which wealth is generated by taking from one another. Indeed, wealth has been created. How much more wealth can be created and circulated if, instead of taking the last mite from the widow, she willingly spends and consumes from her abundance.[197] How much more wealthy could the top one percent be if those at the bottom had more to spend?

We have allowed our entire system to function with no vision beyond the shortsighted benefit of profiting. We have become comfortable within a world which uses capitalism to extract every penny it can from every individual, instead of using it to extract the greatness from every individual, and then generate wealth based on that potential. I believe we have yet to see the true wealth potential of the United States. Achieving this potential would require a shift in the mindset of the government and policy makers. The benevolence needed to be willing to seek the potential of every citizen cannot and should not be expected by the "butcher." This benevolence could, however, be expected of a government seeking to create new levels of wealth never before seen.

Admittedly, this is a utopian fantasy which would first require great theoretical and empirical research to support. However, if we are all dreaming of utopia, would you rather dream of a world which seeks to extract the greatness out of every individual, or one that seeks to extract the last penny from them?

The Verdict

In America, under capitalism, there remains great poverty and injustice. However, there is also great opportunity that could not exist under any other economic system. The vast majority of this opportunity is created by the same economic forces that institutionalizes poverty and incentivizes injustices.[198] Capitalism is neither good nor evil. It is a tool: one that drives our nation's economy and creates jobs and opportunities. It is the only economic model thus far that is capable of creating enough wealth to sustain a global population that is approaching seven billion. Yet, it is far from perfect. It still leaves billions in poverty worldwide. Although capitalism may perpetuate many of the causes of poverty, it is a necessary evil for continued progress and opportunity.

To this end, the government has the responsibility of providing its citizens equal access and opportunity. This ensures that every citizen has an equal chance to prosper in America as any other citizen. Without equal access and opportunity, our economic system will not function to its maximum potential. In other words, we have yet to see the greatness that our nation and our economic engine can achieve if every citizen had an equal opportunity to participate. Finally, the government has a responsibility to protect its citizenry from predatory practices that would rob them of their. Few, if any, citizens have the wherewithal to survive in a society in which corporations, banks, and the wealthy have more power than the government.[199]

All Americans should be leery of any politician, political party, or activist whose primary goal is less regulation and smaller government—one which would leave the citizenry at the mercy of the powerful. Yet, this is exactly what many in the Republican Party advocate for. We have no need for a government that is so powerful that we cannot achieve or enjoy prosperity. However, we cannot deny the value of a government that can ensure equal access to—and protection in—our economic system. Without which, capitalism in America would be akin to the room of children in which the toys are America's resource. Without adult supervision, the strongest, meanest, and most cunning child would control everything without regards to the condition of the others in the room.

10.

THE MORAL IMPERATIVES OF TAXATION

> Why put me to the test, you hypocrites? Show me the coin for the tax.' And they brought him a denarius. And Jesus said to them, 'Whose likeness and inscription is this?' They said, 'Caesar's.' Then he said to them, 'Therefore render to Caesar the things that are Caesar's, and to God the things that are God's.'
> —Matthew 22:18-21 (ESV)

Evangelical Christians have been electing Republican politicians into office for more than a generation with the hopes of Republicans restoring traditional family values. In more than thirty years of promises, little has actually been achieved. Abortions and divorce rates are higher than ever. Families are still breaking apart. American culture is, in many ways, more immoral than it was before Christians began electing Republicans into office. Politicians who promised to bring traditional values back have consistently failed Evangelical voters time and again. However, where these politicians have failed on social issues, they have succeeded in changing tax policy. Since the Christian vote was ultimately used for tax breaks, it is imperative that we understand the moral implications of taxation.

GOD IS NOT A REPUBLICAN

THEOLOGY OF THE TAX

There is indeed a moral element to taxation. From the scripture quoted at the beginning of this chapter, we can extract two aspects of this morality. The first component, found in the scripture in Matthew, is our Christian duty to be subject to the rulers which are in authority:

> Everyone must submit himself to the governing authorities, for there is no authority except that which God has established. The authorities that exist have been established by God.
> —Romans 13:1 (NIV)

Charles Spurgeon, one of the most respected minds in Christian theological thought, uses the Christ's teaching on paying our tribute to Caesar to support the notion that Christianity was not the source of rebellion in a nation. In many ways, Spurgeon believed that Christianity taught believers to be good citizens. He stated:

> Did not our Master say, "Render unto Caesar the things that are Caesar's, and unto God the things that are God's?" Did he not himself pay tribute though he sent to the fish of the sea, to get the shekel? [200]

For Spurgeon, it was not only moral for Christians to pay taxes; it is also a testament to the synthesis of good citizenship and faith.

William Barclay, respected twentieth century theologian, extracted the second element of Christian morality, as it pertains to taxation, from the same scripture that began this chapter. Barclay focused his attention on the coin which Jesus asked the religious leaders to show him. The coin carried the image and inscription of Caesar. The fact that their coin—which was emblematic of all of their wealth—carried the image and inscription of Caesar meant that their wealth was an outgrowth of Caesar's government. In other words, their wealth was not only the product of their profession, training, and hard work, it was also the product of the structure and security Caesar's government provided. They would not have had the coin if not for Caesar's rule. This is evident by the fact that the coin was marked with his image. For Barclay, citizens had a moral obligation to support the government that made it possible for them to obtain the wealth they enjoy. He states:

> Every Christian has a double citizenship. He is a citizen of the country in which he happens to live. To it he owes many things. He owes the safety against lawless men which only a settled government can give; he owes all public services. ... The Christian had a duty to Caesar in return for the privilege, which the rule of Caesar brought to them.[201]

Burden of the Tax

Most Americans cannot imagine living in anarchy, a constant state of war, or the looming fear of uncertainty. The reason we are unable to imagine a society such as this is because of the security our nation provides. While that security is not absolute, we can reasonably live without the fear of a foreign threat or the fear of our neighbor attacking us to take our wealth. This fact cannot be overstated. If not for the security and stability provided by the government, we would be, as Thomas Hobbes stated, "...in the state and posture of gladiators, having [our] weapons pointing, and [our] eyes fixed on one another."[202]

Harvard economist and political theorist, Mancur Olson, labeled all forms of government as stationary "bandits" which provides its "citizens" security and protection from roving bandits. Olson labels them as bandits because every form of government forcibly extracts wealth from its citizens through taxation. Because a *governmental* bandit is stationary, it is able to provide its citizens with security from other bandits. This enables citizens to focus on enterprise and to anticipate their tax burden to the government. Citizens tacitly agree with this structure because of the assurance that they will be able to keep the wealth that remains after taxation. From this perspective, we can consider government as a necessary evil which provides the stability required for economic growth.[203]

Citizens not only benefit from the security the nation provides, we also benefit from the economy that is born from this stability and security. There is no economy in the absence of a government. There is no free enterprise without the stability necessary for citizens to be free to focus on education and entrepreneurship instead of war and survival. To this end, all of our accomplishments, education, and wealth are an outgrowth of the security, stability and opportunity provided by the government. According to the book of Matthew, Christ teaches us that we should pay the appropriate tribute (tax) to the very government that created the framework through which we prospered economically.

Nevertheless, no one looks forward to paying taxes. No matter how patriotic or honorable paying taxes may be, taxes remain a burden for which every citizen shares responsibility. We can debate as to the appropriate size of the government and how much the government should or should not be spending. Regardless of how big or small, we all owe our nation its due tribute. This is both patriotic and biblical. Republican Successes with Tax Policy

Without question, the Republican Party's number one accomplishment since 1980 has been the passage of tax cuts. The election of Ronald Reagan in 1980 marked the beginning of both the coalition between Evangelicals and the Party and the institution of Trickle-Down Economics.[204] Reagan was never able to get the constitutional amendment passed which would have made prayer in schools legal.[205] He was, however,

The Moral Imperatives of Taxation

able to get the Economic Recovery Tax Act of 1981 passed. This legislation cut the top tax bracket from seventy percent to fifty percent and later reduced it to twenty eight percent—a difference of forty-two percentage points.[206] The Moral Majority helped elect Reagan to the presidency to bring morality back to the nation. President Reagan only succeeded at passing tax cuts. His rhetoric was religious His actions were economic.

George W. Bush was elected into office by Evangelical voters in 2000. In the first year of his administration, President Bush was able to sign into law legislation that lowered the top tax bracket from 39.6% to 35%.[207] The tax cuts were hailed as a major economic victory. Bush's administration would have no such victory for social policies. Indeed, most of President Bush's social achievements were merely symbolic in comparison to the success he had in passing the Bush Era tax breaks.

The tax cuts passed by Reagan and Bush have slowly shifted a significant amount of the tax burden away from the wealthiest among us. Where, in the past, the top tax bracket has been as high as ninety-four percent, today it is thirty-five percent.[208] Since the implementation of Republican tax policy, there has been a tremendous shift in the distribution of the American tax burden.

Shifting the Burden

The US tax burden grew exponentially during the same time period that tax revenues declined.[209] This is the reason we find ourselves in the economic condition that we are in today. Indeed, we are faced with a difficult decision. Either we will raise taxes, cut the benefits that the nation provides, or continue to run deficits. If we raise taxes, who do we raise them on: the poor, middle class, wealthy, or businesses? If we cut benefits, whose benefits do we cut. Do we cut Medicare and Social Security? Do we cut social welfare or do we cut corporate welfare? Perhaps the cuts would come from Defense spending. Although our nation has been able to avoid answering these questions for over thirty years by running up the nation's debt, we will eventually be forced to decide which group will pick up the shifted tax burden.

The Morality of the Republican Tax Plan

The Republican Party has made their tax preferences abundantly clear. Members of the Party believe that taxes on businesses and on the wealthiest in our nation should remain low so that this particular demographic can create more wealth for all Americans. Republican tax policy also favors capital over labor. Money made from money—such as investments—is generally taxed at a lower rate than money made from labor—income.[210] This is not an indictment of Republican policy. It is merely an accurate assessment of their policies.

There is nothing inherently wrong with these policies when viewed in isolation. In practice, however, these policies have not clearly produced the economic growth they purported to be able to produce. Wealth was created, but it did not trickle-down.[211] Tax cuts did not inspire job-creators to create jobs.[212] Ultimately, these policies have forced the government to borrow money to sustain itself because they have drained tax revenues from its coffers.

This brings us to the moral imperative of the US tax policy. Who will be responsible for the shifted tax burden that is the direct result of the generation of tax breaks that occurred from Presidents Reagan to Bush? Will the burden be carried by removing the safety nets of Social Security, Medicare and Medicaid, and other programs that ensure that the working poor and the elderly will not fall through the cracks of our nation? Will the burden be carried by raising taxes on the middle class, or by removing programs aimed at helping them move up in our economic strata, or will the burden be carried by raising taxes on the wealthiest in our society? The Republican Party has been consistent in this regard. Many of the currently elected Republican politicians have signed a pledge never to raise taxes under any circumstances.[213] Although no Republican politician has explicitly said so, by refusing to raise taxes on businesses and the wealthiest in our nation they have, by default, determined that the shifted tax burden would either be carried by the poor and the middle class or paid for through deficit spending.

Despite their pledge never to raise taxes, the current generation of Republican politicians has foreshadowed their intentions to raise taxes on the poorest among us. We have heard time and again that over forty-seven percent of Americans do not pay income taxes. Whenever a politician says this, it usually incites "boos" from their audience. This statistic is used by Republicans to advocate for a flat tax. However, what these politicians do not mention to their audience is that the "forty-seven percent" statistic actually includes the elderly living on Social Security income, families that receive tax refunds and wage earners who—although they pay payroll taxes, Social Security, and FICA taxes—do not make enough to pay income taxes. It is not only likely, but a sheer statistical certainty that some of the people booing *those* "forty-seven percent who pay no income taxes" are in actuality booing their own selves.

Notwithstanding the misleading nature of this statistic, the most disturbing part of how it is used the anger this statistic generates towards the poor. The general sentiment created by this particular talking point is that the poor are not carrying their fair share. Indeed, in our modern political discourse the poor are labeled as freeloaders. Republicans present an image of the "overtaxed small business owner" that is carrying the burden of the freeloading pauper. The low-tax movement is now seeking to institute a flat tax which means that all Americans would pay the same percentage in taxes. With the continued help of Christian voters, low-tax advocates may be able to achieve this.

GOD IS NOT A REPUBLICAN

The Immorality of the Flat Tax

According to the scripture in Matthew, Christ teaches that those of us who benefit from Caesar—the government—should likewise pay tribute—taxes—to Caesar. But what of the differences in the *amount* we benefit from the government. It should be clear to any observer that a person making millions of dollars a year derives more benefit from the United States government than a person making $10,000 a year. Although the scripture does not explicitly say this, we still can explore the implications of the question: Would Christ assert that citizens who derive a greater benefit from Caesar's government be responsible for a greater percentage of Caesar's tax burden? Christ does not explicitly say this in the scripture; therefore, we cannot theologically assert this with integrity. Nevertheless, the question is worthy of examination.

The Widow's Mites

I was reminded of the story of the Widow's Mite by the Republican Party's usage of the statistic regarding how many Americans do not pay income taxes. The story is found in the Gospel of Mark:

> And Jesus sat over against the treasury, and beheld how the people cast money into the treasury: and many that were rich cast in much. And there came a certain poor widow, and she threw in two mites...And he called unto him his disciples, and saith unto them, Verily I say unto you, That this poor widow hath cast more in, than all they which have cast into the treasury: For all they did cast in of their abundance; but she of her want did cast in all that she had, even all her living.—Mark 12:41-44 (KJV)

The Moral Imperatives of Taxation

We can extrapolate from this scripture Christ's principle that those who had little and still gave are credited for giving more than those who gave from their abundance. In other words, although the wealthy may have given a greater share, what they gave ultimately came from their abundance. Although the poor may have given a lesser share, what they gave ultimately came from their scarcity.

Some religious and political thinkers interpret this scripture to support a progressive tax system—one which taxes the wealthy at a higher rate than the poor. This is too much of a stretch for me personally. Theological integrity will not allow me to use this scripture to extrapolate a Christian basis for a progressive tax code. It does, however, teach me a simple moral principle: It is biblically inappropriate to denigrate the amount that the poor, working poor and middle class give in taxes in comparison to the amount any other group pays.

The Immorality of the Shifting the Tax Burden

If the Republican Party's fiscal plan is to extract taxes out of everyone, including those who live beneath the poverty line, what actual good would it do for our economy? It is counterintuitive to believe that citizens, who make just enough to survive, could contribute to the economy if they have fewer resources with which to consume because of the shifted tax burden. It is also highly illogical to believe that the tremendous shift in tax burden created by the generation of tax cuts from Reagan to Bush can be sufficiently funded by the poorest among us. If every social program was cut, and taxes were raised on the "forty-seven percent" group, it is unlikely that the hole left by the tax cuts will be filled.

More important than these economic musings; what do these economic goals say about the sense of economic morality in the Republican Party? How could anyone believe it moral to choose to end our social safety net in order to sustain tax breaks for the wealthiest? How could any group that purports to be the representatives of Christ choose to cut social welfare in order to continue corporate welfare? What does it say about Christians that we support the government imposition of biblically based social morality yet say nothing of biblically based economic morality?

11.

THE SECULAR CASE FOR ECONOMIC MORALITY

Throughout this book, we assert that religious and sexual morality should not be forced on society because doing so would be out of line with the freedoms assured by both the Bible and the Constitution. We must be consistent to this principle with regard to economic morality. As tempting as it may be, Christians should not use biblical principles as the sole basis for government enforcement of economic morality. No matter how much enforcing biblically based economic morality may seem to be in line with the principles and spirit of Christ, doing so is equivalent to our fellow Christians advocating for the government to enforce biblically based sexual morality.

While many scriptures lead some Christians to believe that Christ would implement policies aimed at helping the hurting and the poor, policy makers must establish non-religious bases for the implementation of any policy. This is not to say our faith cannot affect policy. It is merely to say that it should not be the sole basis for that policy. Nevertheless, there are many reasons—beyond religion—for the government to enact policies that create an economically moral environment.

GOD IS NOT A REPUBLICAN

Economic Mobility

Many Americans happily work within the confines of capitalism because many Americans still believe that hard work and good decision making moves us up the economic ladder. In fact, according to Pew Research on Charitable Trusts, Americans still believe that all they need in order to get ahead in our nation is effort, intelligence, and skills.[215]

> Economic inequality...is a fact of life and not all that disturbing as long as there is constant movement out of the bottom and a fair shot at making it to the top...Much of what [we] believe about the fairness of the American economy is dependent on the generally accepted notion that there is a high degree of mobility...[214]
> —Isabel Sawhill, Brookings Institution

Economic mobility is the ability of individuals to move up or down in the economic strata. More specifically, it is the ability of our children to move into a higher economic status than they are born into. The higher the mobility of a nation the greater the chance a child born into poverty will be able to move out of poverty and into the middle class.[216] Contrary to popular belief, the United States has low mobility compared to other developed nations.[217] This means that someone born into poverty in the United States is more likely to remain in poverty than someone born into poverty in another developed nation.[218] Poverty is a self-reinforcing cycle that perpetuates itself from one generation to the next.

Too many of us see poverty as not being our problem. However, poverty does not only cripple the person living in poverty; it also cripples the many businesses they cannot afford to patronize. The Great Recession is the best illustration of this. If citizens have less money to spend, businesses and the economy suffer. The true capacity for wealth creation in the economy is never met with a large segment of the nation living in poverty. Francis Fukuyama, political scientist and Standard University Fellow, believed that capitalism worked better with economic mobility and high levels of education. He aptly stated:

> Without universal literacy and education, without a high degree of social mobility and occupations open to talent rather than privilege, capitalist societies would not work, or would not work as efficiently as they could.[219]

OUTCOMES VS. OPPORTUNITY

Should the government guarantee us equal outcomes or merely equal opportunity to participate since capitalism creates unequal results? The generation that defeated communism answered this for us. Attempts to guarantee outcomes change the system from capitalistic to communistic. The majority of America has decidedly rejected the pure socialist and communist economic system.[220] Winston Churchill, British Prime Minister during World War II, stated:

> The inherent vice of capitalism is the unequal sharing of blessings; the inherent virtue of socialism is the equal sharing of miseries.[221]

It is not the role of government to guarantee outcomes. Every person is different with different capabilities; therefore, America will always have those that excel greater than others. It is, however, the opportunity to succeed that matters most. For Americans to accept the realities of capitalism—and the inherent inequalities that it fosters—it is necessary for the government to enact policies aimed at giving all citizens an equal opportunity to participate in the American dream. Without equal opportunity to participate, capitalism guarantees that those who began their life in poverty will more likely remain in poverty. Not only would they remain in poverty, but so too would their children. Opportunity, education, and certainly the wealth of one's parents play a significant role our success and certainly in the success of the next generation.[222]

Today's unresolved debate is over what equal opportunity actually means and how and whether the government can guarantee it. This is where the debate over justice is divided along political lines. Does justice mean equal access and opportunity to obtain prosperity? Is it considered an injustice if all Americans do not have access to opportunities and a fair shot? Should the government not be involved and simply allow the market to make these determinations without any regard for equal access and opportunity?

If all things were left at the mercy of the free market, and charity was left completely to churches and non-profits, we would have a system in which those born into poverty would have very little statistical chance of moving beyond poverty. The economy would miss the productivity of this entire group. The more consumers and producers active in the economy the stronger the economy will be. Therefore, it is always in the best interest of the government to institute policies that create equal opportunity and access to the resources necessary for success. While equal opportunity will never guarantee equal outcomes, it does mean that a person born in abject poverty would have a relatively fair chance at finding success in America in comparison to someone born into privilege.

The Secular Case for Progressive Taxation

Ironically, the best evidence for a progressive tax code comes, not from the Bible, but from Adam Smith—the father of our modern economic system. His classic, *Wealth of Nations*, is most often cited to support free market capitalism and low taxation. However, many readers of Smith either have not read him in his entirety or have chosen to ignore the passages

The Secular Case for Economic Morality

which contradict their particular ideology. With regard to taxation, Smith notes:

> The subjects of every state ought to contribute towards the support of the government, as nearly as possible, in proportion to their respective abilities; that is, in proportion to the revenue which they respectively enjoy under the protection of the state. The expense of government to the individuals of a great nation is like the expense of management to the joint tenants of a great estate, who are all obliged to contribute in proportion to their respective interests in the estate.[223]

In this passage, Smith establishes the principle that our individual rate of taxation should be based on the benefit we derive from the state. Much like Christ's admonition to "Render unto Caesar," Smith suggests that tax rates should be "in proportion to the revenue which they...enjoy under the protection of the state."[224] Nearly two millennia later, Smith not only underscores the Christian principle of Caesar's Tribute, but goes further:

> The necessaries of life occasion the great expense of the poor. They find it difficult to get food, and the greater part of their little revenue is spent in getting it...It is not very unreasonable that the rich should contribute to the public expense, not only in proportion to their revenue, but something more than in that proportion.[225]

Here, Adam Smith, the father and intellectual source for our entire economic system, makes a clear case for a progressive tax system. If the poorest among us are to ever have an opportunity to move up in the economic strata, they will need every penny they can earn. If members of the middle class are ever to have an opportunity to advance, they will need to retain as much of their income as possible to invest into opportunities. Ironically, Republicans understand this principle in regards to "job creators." The Party incessantly advocates for lower taxes on behalf of investors so that they can continue to invest. Does not the same principle hold true for the average citizen?

Money to Make Money

Anyone who has attempted to open a business, further their education, or find a job understands the principle: it takes money to make money. Every successful business person measures a potential business partner based not only on their character, but also on the structure, amount and security of their assets. This principle is only relaxed when we fundamentally tell the poor that they should pull themselves up by their own bootstraps.

By keeping economic resources away from a person born into poverty, we are essentially telling them to make money with no money. We are advising them to get an education even though it now costs thousands of dollars to do so. We are telling them to focus and get good grades when they often have no food in their stomachs. Without allocating resources to those citizens born into poverty, we are telling them to perform at the same level as citizens born into wealth and opportunity without giving them the tools to help them do so. Opportunities in America increase as access to resources and wealth increases.

Taxation for Opportunity

Ensuring that the greatest possible number of citizens participate in the economy is beneficial for the individual and the overall economy. Shifting the tax burden from the wealthiest in our nation to those who can least afford it weakens their opportunity to participate in the economy in a meaningful manner and decreases economic mobility. This makes it more likely that citizens born into poverty will not be able to contribute to the overall economy in a meaningful manner. The proper tax structure helps the nation grow the economy by increasing the number of people participating in the economy. The more citizens able to participate in the economy the stronger the economy will be. The more citizens able to consume products the wealthier the producers of those products will be. Wealth is far more likely to trickle-up as more people move out of poverty and into the middle class than it is to trickle-down from the top.

Capitalism is not about sharing wealth to better the society in which the wealth was gained: it is about harnessing resources in order to create more wealth. However, a proper tax code allows the government not only to provide stability, but also the structure that all citizens benefit from, but also opportunities for more citizens to participate in the creation of wealth.

Voting for Morality or Taxes?

It is our jobs as individuals to take issues that are important to us and advocate on their behalf. For over a generation, the causes that Evangelical Christians brought into the public square were family values and social morality. Evangelicals elected Republicans in hopes seeing legislation enacted to accomplish their goals or morality. However, all they received in return were tax cuts that ultimately put our nation, the middle class, and the poorest among us at a great disadvantage.

The Republican Party's policies have demonstrated that their true loyalties lie with low-tax advocates and not values-voters. For this reason, it is important for Christians to be aware of what their votes are truly being used for. If Evangelical Christians continue to vote for the Republican Party, they should do so with the clear understanding that their votes are less likely to change the morality of the nation and more likely to change the tax-code.

•SECTION 3•
CONSERVATISM

12.

NO OTHER GODS

THE CONSERVATIVE RELIGION

Jerry Falwell spoke of his "hero," Ronald Reagan, in an article he wrote in 2002 as Reagan's health began ailing. In this article, Falwell intertwined conservative political ideologies with Christian values. This seamless integration is the result of thirty years of conflating our faith with politics to the point that today *Republican* and *Evangelical Christian* are all but synonymous terms. Falwell stated in regards to Reagan:

> [H]e was as pro-life, pro-family, pro-national defense and pro-Israel as we were... I appeal to all believers across this nation to rededicate ourselves to the Reagan agenda. Let us fearlessly stand up for the unborn, the biblical family, a strong national defense and unswerving support for Israel.[226]

A Southern Baptist Evangelical Christian pastor using the words "rededicate" in regards to a political commitment to Ronald Reagan is troubling considering Christians are asked to "rededicate" their lives to Christ when appeals are given in church. It is also indicative of the symbiotic relationship between Christianity and the GOP. [227]

GOD IS NOT A REPUBLICAN

Nine years later Falwell's son, Jerry Falwell, Jr. unknowingly revealed the depth of this relationship as he introduced Rick Perry, former presidential candidate and Texas governor, to ten thousand students of Liberty University. Liberty University was founded on Christian principles and was designed to shape the lives of future Christian leaders. As Falwell put it, "The goal [at Liberty] is not only to teach students how to make a living, but also how to live."[228]

Undoubtedly, the lifestyle that Falwell was referring to was based on both Christian values and the life of Christ. Nevertheless, as he introduced Perry, Falwell lifted up the AA bond rating of the university and compared it to the recently downgraded AA+ rating of "President Obama's America" to the delight and the applause of the Christian students. Laughter and applause filled the room as Falwell discussed Rick Perry's gun record as having an AAA rating from the National Rifle Association. The audience of future Christian leaders erupted as their president described Perry's definition of gun control as "hold[ing] a gun with both hands when firing."[229]

Admittedly, Falwell's speech was aimed at humor. Nevertheless, the applause and laughter spoke volumes with respect to the relationship between the Republican Party and the Evangelical Community. It has become increasingly difficult to differentiate between the political ideology of Republicans and the religious principles of Christian leaders. After thirty years of a symbiotic relationship between the GOP and Christianity, it would seem as though the union has given birth to a new faith: one which takes the worst of religion and mixes it with the worst of politics.

Religion in Politics or Politics in Religion

Much has been said about religion being inserted into politics. Religious rhetoric, attempts to legislate morality based on religion, and the mobilization of Christian voters around social issues have all been cited as examples of the influence of religion on contemporary politics. Despite these concerns, the Constitution limits the extent that religion can have on public policy. The Constitution protects both the government from being controlled by religion and religion from being controlled by the government. There is, however, no guarantee which keeps religion from being influenced by politics. In fact, this is exactly the case.

Politics has influenced religion to the extent that it is nearly impossible to delineate between pastors and politicians or between political speeches and sermons. Listening to politically motivated pastors is eerily reminiscent of listening to Republican politicians. Pastors preach about our rights to gun ownership, the need for tax breaks and deliver anti-socialist, anti-communist rhetoric almost as often as their counterparts in the party. Listening to Republican politicians speak is much like listening to passionate televangelists. GOP candidates have learned the value of speaking our language—saying key words that are sure to stir the hearts of anyone who loves Christ. There has been a synthesis of politics and religion at a much deeper level than a mere coalition. What is missing, however, from the political speech of some Republicans is Christ type of love and concern for Christ's constituency: the hurting, poor, sick, and brokenhearted.[230].

> These people draw near Me with their mouths and honor Me with their lips, but their hearts hold off and are far away from Me...for they teach as doctrines the commands of men.
> —Matthew 15:8-9 (AMP)[231]

Then Came Marriage

Jerry Falwell, Jr. did not realize it at the time but he provided, perhaps, the best example of the evolution of the symbiotic relationship between the Evangelical Church and the Republican Party. Instead of Christianity having influence over the Party by letting our light shine, the Party has had influence over Christianity. How many Christians have conformed to the image of the Republican Party by turning a blind eye to the Christian values that contradict the Party platform? How many pastors now preach the virtues of capitalism with no regard to its vices?

What began with several Christian leaders hoping to bring a moral revival to the nation through the Republican Party resulted in a symbiotic relationship in which it is impossible to tell the difference between the host and the parasite. The thirty year relationship has produced a child that inherited religious zealotry, ideological purity, anger-based politics, and economic immorality. So much of the love that Christ had for His fellowman has been removed. This is evident by the celebrations over death and executions as well as the increasing antipathy for both foreigners and the poor. What remains is a new religion that has the form of godliness and the sound of righteousness, but lacks the love and compassion that is core to Christianity. It is the Conservative Religion.

The Conservative Religion is not Christianity. It is not necessarily the Republican Party, the Tea Party, or Conservatism. The Conservative Religion is religious-like devotion to conservative principles at the expense of love and compassion, which are inseverable from Christianity. It is a set of beliefs that have been wholly accepted as statements of faith by its adherents despite any and all evidence to the contrary.

The Conservative Religion is a socio-economic belief system that takes the worst of religion and politics and fuses it with anger. The seeds of this false religion have been planted in the minds of Americans who are sincerely frustrated with the condition of American politics and economy. These frustrations are fueled by politicians, pundits, and strategists who have mastered the art of half-truths. This anger based religion projects antipathy onto the poor and the oppressed. Anger is the only emotion powerful enough to explain how millions of voters consistently vote against their best economic interests.

The Conservative Religion

TENETS OF THE FAITH

There have been several articles written about the Ten Commandments of the Republican Party. Although some of these articles are written in jest, in 2010 the Republican Party issued guidelines that have become a litmus test for any potential candidate based on Ronald Reagan's Unity Principle.[232]

These standards are used to measure the conservative credentials of a Republican candidate. In principle, the Party would only support candidates who affirmed at least seven of these ten principles. However, in practice the litmus test has become much more stringent; candidates are eliminated for not complying with each of the "commandments."[234] In many respects, the following interpretations of conservative principles have become their dogma:

1. Economic policies based on Trickle-Down economics
2. An aggressive and preemptive foreign policy aimed at asserting American values abroad (
3. Social policies aimed at forcing the morality of one group on all Americans (Religious Right)
4. Biblical morality, except when scripture contradicts the economic policy (Sexual Morality without Economic Morality)
5. Promotion of xenophobia[233]
6. Opposition to any science that does not support the politics of the new religion
7. Antagonism against any form of compromise with Democrats or anyone who does not believe in the policies above

GOD IS NOT A REPUBLICAN

Laissez Faire Capitalism
High and Lifted Up

The core tenant of the Conservative Religion is unquestioned devotion to a particular economic theory. The Reality of our economic system is that it is inherently unequal. Yet, if anyone questions capitalism in a meaningful way, or asks questions about the increasing wealth disparity in our nation, they are instantly labeled as socialist or communist. Any attempts at a healthy debate as to how more people can benefit from the system is instantly dismissed as class warfare. Classical and Neoliberal economics have become absolute and unquestionable. More specifically, the Republican interpretation of these theories have become unquestionable not only for their party members, but increasingly so for the general public.

Anger towards God because of our plight in life and even questioning Him are increasingly becoming the norm for believers and non-believers alike.[235] It is not considered a sin to question God or to express disappointment towards Him because of the challenges our lives bring. In fact, some spiritual leaders believe that it is healthy to do so.

If it is acceptable for the faithful to question God, then surely questioning America's economic system should be acceptable. Unfortunately, this is not the case in America. It should concern us as Christians that it is more acceptable for us to question God than it is to question capitalism or the Republican Party. Nevertheless, it would appear that capitalism—Classical theory in particular—holds a higher place in our society than God. Unlike God, it remains unquestionable.

Economics by Faith

Our economic system is accepted by faith by many Americans. Too many accept the infallibility of these systems, not as a result of their personal experience with them, but as a result of years of indoctrination. Even political leaders adopt these principles as absolute and unquestionable. Republicans serving in congress today have signed a pledge stating that they will never raise taxes under any circumstances.[236] They have done this to prove their commitment to the economic tenet of the Conservative Religion. This blind devotion threatens the nation's economic future just as much—if not more—than our out of control national debt.

Faith Minus Love

The Conservative Religion is fixated on sexual morality but requires a blind eye to economic morality. It incorporates religious zealotry into government while simultaneously extracting all notions of charity from government. This subsequently creates a religion that directly opposes one of the greatest principles in Christianity:

> Now abideth faith, hope, charity, these three:
> but the greatest of these is charity.
> —1 Corinthians 13:13 (ESV)

The emotions of sincere Christians are regularly stirred by the rhetoric of "God and Country" along with the public pronouncements of faith by politicians vying for votes. We are made to feel that America will be more Christian if only we banned all forms of abortion and kept gays and lesbians in the closet. The underlying fallacy is simple: if the adherents of the Conservative Religion truly wanted America to be Christian, they could not separate economic morality from any other form or morality. Indeed, Christ preached more about love and charity than he did about sexual morality.

Conservative Heaven

When asked what America would look like if all of her aspirations for the country came to pass, conservative author, Ann Coulter, answered:

> It would look like New York City during the Republican National Convention. In fact, that's what I think heaven is going to look like...happy, joyful, Republicans.[237]

This particular moment exemplifies the difference between the Christians who voted Republican for moral reasons and Republicans who made their political ideology their religion. Notwithstanding the demographic concerns that Coulter's vision of heaven would present, the most troubling aspect of her comment is the ease with which she and other Republican operatives merge their version of Christianity with their political ideology. Although many Americans are familiar with Coulter's unique marketing technique, it is disturbing that she labels those with whom she disagrees as "demonic."[238] This only adds to the religious overtones of the new faith.

What has emerged from the prophets of the new faith is a political ideology that now carries the absolutism that is usually only found in religion:

> We are right.
>
> Those that do not believe what we teach are wrong.
>
> Things will be better once the infidels are all gone.
>
> We must never compromise our principles.
>
> This is God's will.

These are not the words of Islam, Judaism, or Christianity. These are the words of The Conservative Religion. While this new religion is not Christianity or necessarily the Republican Party, it poses a threat to both.

THREAT TO THE REPUBLICAN PARTY

The purity tests which Republican candidates have been held to have pushed the Party further to the Right than ever before. While the most extreme elements of both political parties traditionally sustained the party over time, it has always been necessary for each to appeal to moderate voters in order to obtain political power. In this regard, both parties have had to be somewhat moderate in the past. Radicalism may have its place, but it rarely gets into power. Despite the abundance of rhetoric from both sides, the majority of America remains moderate.

This presents a problem for the Republican Party establishment. The new religion forces every Republican candidate further to the right. It appears as though in order for any Republican to receive support from the base he or she must espouse the extreme views of the faith. Most analysts agree that a Conservative—by today's standards—could never win the majority of the nation's votes. The same would be true of a truly extreme liberal candidate. Moderation has its place in American politics.

THREAT TO CHRISTIANITY

The Conservative Religion also poses a tremendous threat to Christianity. It requires that believers ignore the core Christian value of love from their political beliefs. The danger arises when Christians allow their politics to affect their faith. When we separate from the practice of Christianity the love, acceptance, and charity that Christ demonstrated, all that is left is self-righteousness, hypocrisy, and religious dogma.

When we conform our religion to a particular political ideology, whether Conservative or Liberal, we weaken the message of Christ. When that political ideology causes us to forget Christ's commandment to love one another, we weaken the power of our faith. When our politics forces us to turn a blind eye to the inherent inequities of our economic system so that we can be compliant with our political allegiances, then our politics has had a greater influence on our faith than our faith has had on our politics. Christ did not call us to spread laissez-faire capitalism; He called us to spread the Gospel. If our commitment to the Republican economic platform is greater than our commitment to love and charity, then our Christianity has been subverted by the Conservative Religion.

The threat to our faith is clear: the more our faith is used to justify a particular economic or political ideology, the more validity our faith loses. The more our politics causes us to turn a blind eye to our duty to give both love and charity, the more validity our faith loses. We were charged with being the salt of the world, able to change any environment we enter. Instead, the environment has changed us. How can America ever see the power of Christ in our faith if that faith is a wholly owned subsidiary of the Republican Party?

In many ways, the Republican Party establishment placed the character and person of Christ into the political debate. By doing this, they exposed Him to the same vitriol that every public figure must endure. Indeed, Christ has been politicized. However, the Conservative Religion is a much greater threat and does much more damage to our faith than simply politicizing Christ. The Conservative Religion reaches *into* our belief system and attempts to change the very essence of our faith. It attempts to remove the Christ-like love which would otherwise require that we open our eyes and see the blatant inequities of our economic and political system. This same Christ-based love necessarily requires that we do something about what we see. Without the distinctive element of love, our religious words are nothing more than rhetoric:

> If I could speak all the languages of earth and of angels, but did not love others, I would only be a noisy gong or a clanging cymbal.
>
> —1 Corinthians 13:1 (NLT)

The Conservative Religion

What is Christianity without love? It applauds Rick Perry's execution score card as though the death penalty could be taken as lightly as a child's game.[239] It boos an American soldier who put his life on the line for our freedoms simply because he was gay.[240] It is an audience that laughs when three audience members shout, "Yeah," to letting people without healthcare die.[241] It indulges in anger, bitterness, and confusion. Christianity without love is not Christianity: it is a political tool. It is the Conservative Religion.

I fear that if Christians continue to indulge in this perversion of our true faith, we will miss the days when people simply *disliked* us because they believed we were controlled by the Republican Party. Their disdain for us will lead them to hate Christ because of how we misrepresented Him. There were occasions in history when men and women needed to be delivered from persecution suffered at the hands of religious zealots. This is true even for Christianity. If we as Christians continue to allow our true faith to be co-opted by blind allegiance to the conservative political ideology, we may soon discover that the world will need to be delivered from Christianity because of the injustices, persecution, and oppression dealt in the name of Christ for political gain.

It may be unreasonable to assert that the union between conservatism and evangelicalism has emerged as a new religion. However, consider the evidence. Followers cling to the political tenets which must be accepted with blind faith and unquestioned devotion. This religion has gone so far as to create a variation of "heaven" in the minds of some of its adherents—based on the demographics and ideology of conservatism. This belief system is heralded as the "only way" to save our nation. Finally, anyone who does not adhere to these beliefs is labeled as "lost" at best and "demonic" at worst. It may be a stretch to consider this a new religion, but it is far from unreasonable to analyze it as such.

13.

Conservative Contradictions

There are some evangelicals who cannot understand how a Christian could vote for the Democratic Party. Likewise, there are other Christians who cannot understand how Evangelical Christians can vote with the Republican Party because of the glaring contradictions that exist between who Christ was and the party platforms of the GOP. Some of the planks in the platform are opposed to Christian principles. Although no political party is remotely capable of representing Christ in His entirety, many Christians have adopted these contradictory party platforms into our belief system. The greatest tragedy is the attempt to use the Bible to justify policies that are clearly un-Christian.

War and Peace

One of the biggest conservative contradictions is the usage of Christ, the Prince of Peace, to wage war. Clearly occasions arise for which our nation must go to war. However, no matter how just a war may be, using Christ, Christianity, or religious language to garner support for the campaign is insulting to our faith. Many military historians, scholars, and leaders understand as stated by Carl Von Clausewitz, "war is nothing more than the continuation of politics by other means."[242] Wrapping it in religious terms has historically been the medium through which to gain popular support and has led to tragic results throughout history.

GOD IS NOT A REPUBLICAN

This technique is to be expected from political leaders. Whatever the true cause of the conflict, they must gain popular support if they are to wage a successful conflict. "This is just what politicians do."[243] Nevertheless, we must expect more from the clergy. It is not in the job description of pastors to use biblical terminology to support US war policy. Pastors should be free to preach whatever they wish according to their doctrines; however, using Christ to gain political favor, especially when this means using the Prince of Peace to justify war, is clearly a contradiction of whom Christ was:

> For every boot of the tramping warrior in battle tumult and every garment rolled in blood will be burned as fuel for the fire. For unto us a child is born, to us a son is given; and the government shall be upon his shoulders, and his name shall be called Wonderful Counselor, Mighty god, Everlasting Father, Prince of Peace.
> —Isaiah 9:5-6 (ESV)

Here, Isaiah explicitly records that conquest through military violence will end because of the coming of the Prince of Peace. While we still live in a world in which certain threats must be met with force, it is heretical for any religious leader to use religiosity to support or endorse violent conflict.

GOD, GUNS, AND RHETORIC

One of the most glaring conservative contradictions is the synthesis of God and guns. While there are no biblical objections to Christian gun ownership, religion and guns are certainly an unlikely duo. For Christians, the use of violent force should be taken with the utmost reluctance when we consider Christ's many teachings on peace:

> But I say unto you, Love your enemies, bless them that curse you, do good to them that hate you, and pray for them which despitefully use you, and persecute you. —Matthew 5:34 (KJV)

> But I say unto you, that you resist not evil: but whosoever shall smite you on your right cheek, turn to him the other also. —Matthew 5:39 (KJV)

Clearly we can own guns and still treat our enemies with the standard that Christ set during the Sermon on the Mount. However, a predisposition towards violent rhetoric and retribution often permeates conservative political ideology. We see this in political debates, town hall meetings, and in the political language that is used to stir up the conservative base.

To be fair, there is a vast amount of violent speech on both sides of the political spectrum. However, this does not excuse the blatant contradiction of Christians who wear their faith as a badge of honor, only later to use violent political language. Religious justification of this type of behavior requires us to ignore who Christ was and what He stood for.

We are all capable of falling into a moment of heated, angry debate, lashing out with words or actions that are hurtful and even violent. However, the entire point of our Christian faith is that we must resist these moments of temptation. It is through the power of God that we learn to treat our enemies as we would treat ourselves. We were never called to destroy our enemies with words or weapons, all in Jesus' name.

Celebrating Death

Christians and pro-life advocates champion the cause of thousands of babies that are aborted daily in the United States. Yet, their allegiance to the Republican Party simultaneously aligns them with pro-capital punishment policies. We have now seen the transformation of the Republican Party from being a group that supports capital punishment as a necessary evil into one that celebrates the execution score cards of governors as though the death penalty were a video game.[244] This should be unacceptable to every Christian that understands the Bible and understands the value of Life.

It is a disturbing contradiction for Christians to oppose abortion while celebrating the death penalty. While many Christians reject this notion because they believe that unborn children are innocent and that inmates sentenced to death are guilty, DNA has exonerated hundreds of convicted felons; many of which were on death row.[245] Despite the mistakes that are often made by our judicial system, we have seen a new trend in the Republican Party of celebrating the number of inmates governors have executed.

The church is divided on the death penalty debate. While the Catholic Church opposes capital punishment in a consistent appreciation of the gift of life, the Southern Baptist issued a proclamation in support of the death penalty.[246] Regardless of differences, as Christians we all believe that God's grace is sufficient to forgive the worst among us.

> I tell you, her sins--and they are many--have been forgiven, so she has shown me much love. But a person who is forgiven little shows only little love. —Luke 7:47 (NLT)

Every Christian understands what it means to be exonerated and to have our death sentence commuted. Is this not exactly what Christ did for each of us? Was not the wage of our sins death?[247] As Christians, we should be willing to give the guilty among us as much grace as God has shown us. We should also go one step further and extend to them the amount of grace we would need if God had not changed our lives.

These contradictions are not meant to condemn conservative or conservative Christians. It only serves as another example of why it is impossible for a political party or ideology to represent our faith. What Christ expects from us is inconceivable and perhaps laughable to many people who do not know Christ. This is to be expected by those who are not of our faith. We should not accept the distortion of our faith for the purposes of conforming to a political ideology.

•SECTION 4•
THE ROLE OF CHRISTIANITY IN AMERICA

14.

FAITH OF A PRESIDENT

> [N]o religious test shall ever be required as a qualification to any office or public trust under the United States.
> Article VI, Paragraph 3 United States Constitution

During the 1960 Presidential Election, Protestant Americans were extremely concerned with the prospect of electing a Catholic president. They feared his presumed allegiance to the Pope and the Catholic Church. Although John F. Kennedy was never known for being pious, the mere fact that he was a Catholic troubled many of the Protestant pastors of the day.[248] This seems strange today in light of the current political alliance that many Catholics and Evangelicals share. However, it was not until after he gave his speech in September 1960 at the Rice Hotel in Houston that Kennedy was able to lay the issue to rest. He assuaged the fears of most of the protestant pastors when he stated:

> [Because] I am a Catholic, and no Catholic has ever been elected President, the real issues in this campaign have been obscured... So it is apparently necessary for me to state once again—not what kind of church I believe in, for that should be important only to me—but what

GOD IS NOT A REPUBLICAN

> kind of America I believe in. I believe in an America where the separation of church and state is absolute—where no Catholic prelate would tell the president (should he be Catholic) how to act, and no Protestant minister would tell his parishioners for whom to vote.[249]

Fifty years have passed, and questions of presidential faith have resurrected. Over fifty percent of Americans do not believe or are unsure of whether President Barack Hussein Obama is a Christian.[250] Despite the president's constant statements regarding his faith, many Americans refuse to take him at his word. Perhaps this is because his father was from Kenya and was a Muslim before becoming an atheist, or perhaps it is because the President's name is *Barack Hussein Obama*. Regardless of the reason, the majority of Americans do not take President Obama at his word when he says he is a Christian. Included in this number are Americans that may not understand what is required to be a Christian, those who believe the president may be atheist or Muslim, and other Christians who do not accept President Obama's statement of faith.

REQUIREMENTS OF CHRISTIANITY

> If you confess with your mouth that Jesus is Lord and believe in your heart that God raised him from the dead, you will be saved.
> —Romans 10:9 (NLT)

Week in and week out, pastors tell new converts the wonderful news that all they need for salvation is confession, repentance, and belief according to Romans 10:9. In fact, it is this simplicity that is the hallmark of our faith. While the confession of faith can be verified, none of us can truly confirm what an individual truly believes in their heart. Yet, this does not stop us from welcoming these individuals into the family of Christ.

It should concern every Christian if President Obama's faith cannot be accepted based on his public confession of faith.[251] If his confession is not sufficient evidence, then what of our own? The very basis of our faith is our public confession coupled with sincere belief in our hearts. But since no man can judge the heart of another all we can do is accept each person at their word.

Franklin Graham, son of Billy Graham, stated that he could not be certain of President Obama's salvation because he does not know the president's heart. In that same interview, Franklin said that he firmly believed that presidential candidates Rick Santorum and Newt Gingrich were Christians because their confessions were persuasive and because of their actions.[252] What actions could ensure the salvation of one professed Christian and not another professed Christian?

> Whosoever therefore shall confess me before men, him will I confess also before my Father which is in heaven. —Matthew 10:32 (KJV)

Thankfully, Christ's judgment is infinitely fairer and wiser than that of Franklin Graham and other evangelical leaders who refuse to accept President Obama's profession of faith. His standard is clear: He will confess before God those that confessed Him before men.

PHONY THEOLOGY

In February 2012, President Obama delivered a brief speech at the White House annual prayer breakfast. In this speech, the president discussed his spiritual progression and the biblical influences in his political life:

GOD IS NOT A REPUBLICAN

> [When] I talk about our financial institutions playing by the same rules as folks on Main Street, when I talk about making sure insurance companies aren't discriminating against those who are already sick, or making sure that unscrupulous lenders aren't taking advantage of the most vulnerable among us, I do so because I genuinely believe it will make the economy stronger for everybody. But I also do it because I know that far too many neighbors in our country have been hurt and treated unfairly over the last few years, and I believe in God's command to "love thy neighbor as thyself."[253]

Immediately after this speech, Republicans along with some Christians began to discount the president's interpretation of the Bible as erroneous. The Internet immediately began to swarm with allusions to Satan manipulating Christ while He fasted in the wilderness.[254] President Obama's theology was labeled as erroneous at best and phony at worst.[255]

But what if the average Christian were to read the transcript from that day without knowing who gave the speech? Would so many have labeled the underlying theology as erroneous? Would they consider it heretical if an anonymous speaker used the verse, "To whom much is given much is required," as a justification of asking more from the rich in order to help the poor? Chances are they would not have. Nothing the president said was so theologically unsound that it would be labeled as erroneous or heretical by unbiased listeners. If anything the president can be accused of using an eisegetical[256] interpretation of the Bible. This is looked down upon in theological circles, but it is far from heretical. In fact, every Sunday across America, there are pastors who "read into" the text more than it explicitly says in order to convey a point that nonetheless may have validity.

Fear of Association

Although he may not be able to expound as accurately or prolifically as Charles Spurgeon, the president confessed Christ, said that he prays on a daily basis and clearly is a family man.[257] Nevertheless, many in the Religious Right refuse to accept President Obama as a Christian. To do so would mean that the President shares some of the same values as millions of Republican voters. So, then, he is cast in the light of being Muslim or even the Antichrist. There is a tremendous amount of abject fear that surrounds our president. This fear is spread and endorsed by Christian and Republican leaders. The foundation of this fear is sustained by the persistent questioning of his faith.

But why do some Christians refuse to accept a decent, moral family man, and a publicly-confessed Christian, as actually being a Christian? Perhaps it is because the paranoid fear of him would diminish if Christians ever saw him as a brother in Christ. If President Obama is seen by the masses as a Christian, it would instantly create a connection with fellow Christians. This is what many Republican and Religious leaders want to avoid.

Allowing Christians to see the president as a fellow Christian will force many to grapple with the nuances of how the President's faith can allow him to be pro-choice and to support gay-rights. In their eyes, the President could not be a Christian because he is an enemy of the state: a foreigner, socialist, communist, Maoist, Leninist and fascists.[258] He is anything and everything that the Republican Party needs him to be in order to keep him away from their Christian voting bloc. He is anything they need him to be in order to defeat him. And because the GOP depends so much on the Christian vote, they are even willing to exclude President Obama from the Body of Christ.

Perhaps, if the electorate were to see President Obama as being as much of a Christian as former President Bush, the alliance between the GOP and the Evangelical Church would begin to flounder. As much as we celebrated the faith of Bush, we should celebrate the faith of Obama. As much as we looked to Bush to be our great moral leader, so too should we look to the current president. Indeed, the only difference between the faith of Presidents Bush and President Obama is their political stance on abortion and gay rights. In other words, there is no difference in their faith, merely a difference in their politics.

This is perhaps the clearest example of how we as Christians have allowed politics to undermine our definition of Christianity. If Romans 10:9 is what Christians use to determine the salvation of another person, then we must accept that President Obama is a Christian. Not only is he a Christian, he is also a praying family man. Anyone who rejects this notion cannot be doing so based on biblical grounds.

If we as Christians begin splitting hairs of denominationalism, then the faith of the entire Body of Christ will become suspect as we begin having the debate of "our church is right and yours is wrong." These nuances are the very reason there are so many divisions in the faith and complicate the simplicity of salvation.

Double Standards

If the President's faith is such a major issue for many evangelical conservatives, how could they tacitly or expressly support the nomination of Mitt Romney as the Republican Party presidential candidate? Most protestant pastors and theologians believe that Mormonism is not Christianity.[259] Dr. Robert Jeffress, pastor of a 10,000 member Texas mega church, went as far as to call Mormonism a cult.[260] But when asked whether he would support Mitt Romney in the 2012 election over President Obama he stated:

> Given the choice between a non-Christian like Mitt Romney, who at least embraces some biblical positions like the sanctity of life and

sanctity of marriage, as opposed to a professing Christian like Barack Obama, who takes unbiblical positions, I believe there is merit in choosing the non-Christian over the Christian.[261]

Dr. Jefress represents a group of Christians who would vote for a candidate whom *they* have labeled as non-Christian over a professed Christian who says that he prays on a regular basis for God's guidance.[262] In this case, the justification is over differing political positions on abortion and gay-rights.[263] Dr. Jefress is not the official representative of Evangelical Christians; however, if evangelicals believe as he does—that it is better to vote for a non-Christian who is anti-abortion and anti-gay marriage—we must ask ourselves a very important question. How could any Christian use the manufactured doubt of the President Obama's faith to justify the bitter opposition of him while simultaneously being willing to vote for someone most Evangelical pastors believe is not a Christian?

If the faith of the President is a preeminent concern, would it not only be logical for Christians to vote for their fellow Christian over someone they have labeled as non-Christian? If Christians do as Dr. Jefress suggests and turn a blind eye to their faith in order to support someone who espouses a particular political ideology, then have not they elevated two politics above what it actually means to be a Christian and even above salvation itself? Is not anything we lift up above Christ idolatry?[264]

Perhaps the case is much simpler than the preceding paragraph suggests. Perhaps Dr. Jefress meant that the religious affiliation of a president should not matter as much as his political ideology. If this is what Dr. Jefress meant, then I wholeheartedly agree. However, evangelical pastors cannot have it both ways. Either the faith of the President is of utmost importance—in which case they could not support a candidate whom *they* have already labeled as non-Christian—or the faith of the President is not of the utmost importance—in which case their manufactured fear of President Obama should cease. Great confusion arises when we selectively choose when to impose religious standards in the political process.

What If?

What if the president was not Christian? What if he were a Muslim or an Atheist? It is safe to say that one day America will have a president who prays towards Mecca or one that celebrates Hanukkah rather than Christmas. No matter how unlikely it may seem now, as long as America continues, we will eventually have an atheist president.[265] Constitutionally speaking, it does not matter what the religious belief of an individual is. In order to preserve their religious freedoms, the founders had to preserve and protect the religious freedom of all Americans.

What would we do as Christians if America elects someone of another faith to the presidency? Would we rebel because we believe that America is no longer a Christian nation in our eyes? Would we refuse to follow the leadership of a non-believer? Would we challenge the results of the election and claim that, "radical human secularists" manipulated the voting process? What would we do as Christians when this eventuality occurs?

> Everyone must submit himself to the governing authorities, for there is no authority except that which God has established. The authorities that exist have been established by God.
> —Romans 13:1 (NIV)

Here, in Romans, the Bible instructs Christians to obey the authorities in power. It does not distinguish between Christian authority and non-Christian authority. Therefore, when in the face of having a president who is not Christian, we must still obey that authority in power. This scripture has been dismissed as referring to those with religious authority over us, eighteenth century theologian, William Newell, clarified this when he stated:

> Remember your Savior suffered under Pontius Pilate, one of the worst Roman governors Judea ever had; and Paul under Nero, the worst Roman Emperor. And neither our Lord nor His Apostle denied or reviled the authority! [266]

Therefore, both biblically and constitutionally, it should not matter whether the president of the United Sates is a Christian. What would matter, however, is whether that elected official abides by the Constitution because the Constitution is ultimately our governing authority.

The Bible commands that we obey the law of the land and, by extension, its duly elected officials. Likewise, we have the right to oppose any administration—secular or Christian—that violates the Constitution. Any Christian attempting to force religious beliefs on non-believers is in as much violation of the Constitution as any secularists whose aim is to have freedom from religion versus freedom of religion. We have biblical and constitutional grounds to oppose either.

The Common Bonds of the Faithful

There is, of course, value in having some common bonds with the occupant of the White House. There is something to be said about sharing the same religious beliefs as the president. It gives us some sense of common identity and shared values. To know that the president prays to the same God we pray to, shares our same values, and loves Christ just as we do is a great reward to the family of Christ. I can understand the Christian desire to have a president who operates in the love of Christ and who, like us, is a friend of God.

Yet, this is the very gift that we deny ourselves when we refuse to accept President Obama's pronouncement of faith and choose to exclude him from the common bonds that all Christians share. We do not rob the president of this experience. We rob ourselves of it. Those who do not accept him as a Christian for whatever reason fail to see that, despite our political differences, we all have the most important thing in common: Christ Jesus.

15.

FAITH OF OUR FATHERS

One of the longest ongoing debates in our nation deals with the faith of our Founding Fathers and the nation they formed. On the one hand, many Christians assert that America was founded on Christian principles and as a Christian nation. On the other, many believe that America was at a minimum founded as a religion-neutral nation. While the Constitution makes it clear that the government could never make laws establishing a state religion, many Christians cite the faith of the Founding Fathers as evidence that Christianity has a special role in our nation.

If we were to examine the individual faiths of our Founding Fathers by the standard of Romans 10:9, then we must examine their written words for public professions of faith. The dilemma with this type of examination is that each of the Founding Fathers said things that made it clear they believed in Jesus, only to say things at different points in time which made their faith seem ambivalent at best. Below are sayings from several Founding Fathers. For each founder, there is a statement of faith and a statement against religion.

GOD IS NOT A REPUBLICAN

George Washington

Statement of Faith:

> No people can be bound to acknowledge and adore the Invisible Hand which conducts the affairs of men more than the people of the United States. Every step by which they have advanced to the character of an independent nation seems to have been distinguished by some token of providential agency.[267]

Statement against Religion:

> Religious controversies are always productive of more acrimony and irreconcilable hatreds than those which spring from any other cause....I was in hopes that the enlightened and liberal policy, which has marked the present age, would at least have reconciled Christians of every denomination so far that we should never again see the religious disputes carried to such a pitch as to endanger the peace of society.[268]

James Madison

Statement of Faith

> It is the duty of every man to render to the Creator such homage and such only as he believes to be acceptable to him. [269][270]

Statement against Religion

> What influence...have ecclesiastical establishments had on society?...[T]hey have been seen to erect a spiritual tyranny on the ruins of the civil authority...[T]hey have been seen upholding the thrones of political tyranny...Rulers who wish to subvert the public liberty may have found an established clergy convenient auxiliaries. A just government, instituted to secure and perpetuate it, needs them not.[271]

THOMAS JEFFERSON

Statement of Faith

> God who gave us life gave us liberty. Can the liberties of a nation be secure when we have removed a conviction that these liberties are the gift of God?[272]

Statement against Religion

> Millions of innocent men, women and children, since the introduction of Christianity, have been burnt, tortured, fined, imprisoned; yet we have not advanced an inch towards uniformity. What has been the effect...? To make one half the world fools, and the other half hypocrites. To support roguery and error all over the earth.[273]

GOD IS NOT A REPUBLICAN

JOHN ADAMS

Statement of Faith

> I have therefore thought fit to recommend...the 9th day of May next, be observed throughout the United States as a day of solemn humiliation, fasting, and prayer; that the citizens of these States...offer their devout addresses to the Father of Mercies agreeably to those forms or methods which they have severally adopted as the most suitable and becoming; that all religious congregations do, with the deepest humility, acknowledge before God the manifold sins and transgressions with which we are justly chargeable as individuals and as a nation, beseeching Him at the same time, of His infinite grace, through the Redeemer of the World, freely to remit all our offenses, and to incline us by His Holy Spirit to that sincere repentance and reformation which may afford us reason to hope for his inestimable favor and heavenly benediction [274]

Statement against Religion

> The divinity of Jesus is made a convenient cover for absurdity. Nowhere in the Gospels do we find a precept for Creeds, Confessions, Oaths, Doctrines, and whole cartloads of other foolish trumpery that we find in Christianity.[275]

BENJAMIN FRANKLIN

Statement of Faith

> I cannot conceive...that He, the Infinite Father, expects or requires no worship or praise from us, but that He is even infinitely above it.[276]

Statement against Religion

> I wish it (Christianity) were more productive of good works...I mean real good works...not holyday keeping, sermon-hearing...or making long prayers, filled with flatteries and compliments despised by wise men, and much less capable of pleasing the Deity.[277]

AN EXERCISE IN FUTILITY

We can continue this exercise for each of the Founding Fathers. Each of them spoke words that would make some believe they were Christian and with the same mouths uttered words that seemed to refute their faith. Even during their day, many of them were accused of being deists or atheists. Therefore, it is misleading and disingenuous for anyone to assert that the Founding Fathers were Christians as we define Christianity today.

Each of the Founding Fathers had a passion for Christ, His character, morals, and teachings. This is evident by the words they left behind. But each of them also saw the damage that organized religion was capable of inflicting. This ambivalence towards their own religion was the result of their understanding of manipulation of Christendom throughout history. They understood the manipulation that went on not only in churches, but also in politics.

GOD IS NOT A REPUBLICAN

Does it Matter?

Why is it so important to people to prove or disprove whether the founders were Christian? If they were Christians, they clearly created a system to protect their faith by ensuring that all faiths were protected. They knew that Christianity would flourish along with other religions as long as the government did not attempt to assert the tenets of any religion with the force of law. If they were not Christian, they clearly understood the value that faith brings to society. As ambivalent as their faith may have been, they insisted that religion be protected from the government, secularists, and even from itself.

Christianity's Place in America

While we cannot say that America was founded to *be* a Christian nation, we can say that the majority of America *was* Christian at the founding. This, more than anything else, is the reason that Christianity has had a prominent and prestigious role in American culture. And as long as the Body of Christ continues to grow, Christianity will always play a significant role in our culture.

There is no need for us to force our faith, morals, or ideologies on the nation through politics or legislation. The glorious light of the Gospel will always shine brightly enough if it is not clouded by our politics or personal sins. The removal of the Ten Commandments from courtrooms across the country does not weaken our place in society more than our own shortcomings as believers. The removal of prayer in school does not tarnish our image as much as national controversies of pastors and bishops found guilty of fraud, infidelity, and even molestation.

Atheists, agnostics, human secularists, and adherents of other faiths are not our enemies; therefore they cannot be our greatest enemies. We are our own worst enemy. And as long as we are preoccupied with trying to keep these groups from having a seat at the table of democracy and equality, we will continue to be distracted from the things we should be doing to ensure that the seat that has been ours is a seat that is honored and respected because of the light that shines from within us.

16.

CONCLUSION:

TRUE CHRISTIANITY IN POLITICS

IF I BE LIFTED UP

> And I, if I be lifted up from the earth, will draw all men unto me. —John 12:32 (KJV)

These words of Christ carried two generally accepted and significant meanings. The first meaning is in regards to Christ's crucifixion. As He would be lifted up on the cross, the work of salvation would draw all men who believe unto him. Many theologians agree that the second meaning of "lifted up" is in regards to Christian's lifting up the message of the cross and spreading the Gospel.

There is a problem with this scripture: in no way do we see "all men" being drawn to Christ. The scripture did not say "all Christians" or "all potential Christians." It simply said, "all men." What we do see is great antipathy not only for Christians but also for Christ.

Many believers have gone under the belief that the world was destined to hate them because they have first hated Christ:

GOD IS NOT A REPUBLICAN

> All men will hate you because of me, but he who stands firm to the end will be saved.
> —Matthew 10:22 (NIV)

Although there are those who despise Christ and Christians, this does not give us the biblical authority to carry ourselves in a manner which provokes the hatred of all men. In fact, many of us have completely forgotten that by lifting up Christ, all men would be drawn to Him and, subsequently, to the believers. How can they ever be drawn to Christ if Christians are hated and despised, not because of Christ but because of the way we portray Him and carry ourselves?

Presently, it would appear that the scripture in Matthew, regarding the hatred of Christians, is truer than the one of Christ drawing all men unto Him. But is this hatred merely because we *are* Christians or because we are like Christ, or is it the case that, the animosity and hatred focused towards Christians is because of the type of political religion that we have warped Christianity into being? Unfortunately, the latter seems to be truer. They do not hate us because of Christ; they hate Christ because of us.

The Essence of Christ

I believe there is a third meaning of "lifted up" in the scripture. It is one that we too often overlook. The *force* that has the ability to draw all men is not only the message of Christ—the Gospel—but also the person, character, teachings, and essence of Christ. Even the staunchest atheist recognizes the unquestionable character of Jesus. There is no denying the value of His teachings and the positive impacts they can have on one's life. The characteristics which He personified are the traits we seek to imitate.

How else could the world ever be drawn to Him unless we demonstrate the character of Christ? Christians lifting up the essence of Christ through our individual lives has the greatest potential of drawing all men unto Him. This is so much more than having a magnetic personality. It is demonstrating the love, patience, and wisdom of Christ. It is also offering to others the same grace that Christ gave us.

The irony of this scripture is that the only "Jesus" we can lift up is the "Jesus" inside of each of us. We are the only "Jesus" the world sees. If we want the world to be drawn to Christ, they must first be drawn to the *Christ* in us. We cannot afford to allow our brand of political religion to turn people away from Christ.

We have to be the best representatives Christ because we are the only representatives of Christ. Where many of our actions in the past has given Christianity a bad name, we must intentionally show the world that true Christians are peacemakers that are also loving, joyful, patient, kind, faithful, gentle, and have self-control. These are the characteristics we must "lift up" if we are to "lift up" Christ. We must show them that we are like Christ. We must show them what it is to be a true Christian.

> But the fruit of the Spirit is love, joy, peace, longsuffering, gentleness, goodness, faith, meekness, temperance: against such there is no law.—Galatians 5:23 (KJV)

Against Which There is No Law

While we have been distracted by issues such as abortion and gay marriage, we have neglected the set of Christian characteristics that can be asserted in every aspect of our political system: love, joy, peace, patience, kindness, goodness, faithfulness, gentleness, and self-control.[278] These Christian values have the ability to saturate every aspect of our nation. In fact, they have the potential to overtake the entire world because, as the scripture states, there are no legal grounds to oppose them. Most importantly, no politician or party could ever oppose legislation that, at the core, is based on these values or based on instilling these values. This is the unstoppable form of Christianity. This is the form of our faith that we have every liberty and incentive to spread.

Which nation would be more like Christ: one that forces prayer in schools, bans abortions and homosexuality or one that exemplifies the fruits of the Spirit? The former would have the appearance of piety, but not the power of Christ. The former forces people to live in a manner in which they do not willingly wish to live. This is not Christianity.

In every way, the latter would be more like Christ. There have always been opportunities to enhance the character of our nation by first enhancing our own. Unfortunately, too many of us have focused on telling others how they are wrong instead of realizing that we needed to first change in ourselves. True Christianity is not defined merely by what we oppose but by essence of our character.

If we as Christians spent more time examining ourselves and purging those characteristics and habits that were not like Christ, we would realize that there would be no time left to condemn anyone else to hell. We would be too busy working out our own salvation.[279] But if we were ever to become actual Christians, instead of just carrying the title, the world would be changed because there would be a sudden influx of hundreds of millions of people living like Christ!

"I Told You So" Faith

It would seem as though some Christians find it enjoyable to be hated by society; indulging in a vindictive form of Christianity which looks forward to the day that they can look back onto Earth as they are being raptured away, and as billions are being tortured and persecuted say, "I told you so." This form of Christianity is nothing like Christ. There should be no pleasure found in condemning someone to hell no matter what they have done.

If we truly believe that billions of people who do not believe in Christ are destined to suffer in eternal damnation, then those with the love of Christ should be grieving now for such a tragedy. Not only should we be demonstrating grief, but we should be busy living like Christ and showing the love of Christ so that the world would be drawn to Him through us.

POLITICAL TESTIMONIES FROM THE BIBLE

The best biblical examples of how Christians should carry themselves in a nation that is not Christian would be the stories of Joseph, Daniel, and the three Hebrew boys. Each of them was imprisoned in nations that did not know or honor God. Each of them made their way to the top of the political structure while maintaining their faith in secular nations. There are many lessons in their stories that demonstrate the power of true Christianity in a secular political system.

JOSEPH[280]

Joseph was sold as a slave and delivered into Egypt. He was a young man in a covenant with God. Yet, he was enslaved in a pagan land. It was his character that found him favor with Potiphar which led to his promotion from being a slave to being the personal aide to a top official in the Egyptian government. Amid controversy, Joseph maintained his character and remained true to his religious beliefs. Although the controversy led him to being imprisoned, Joseph's character and gifts made a place for him in positions higher than ever before. Once again he was promoted, but this time he moved into the second highest position in all of Egypt.

Joseph was promoted each time because of his character and his ability. Potiphar and the Pharaoh both trusted Joseph because of his integrity. What is more, both of these secular political leaders recognized that the uniqueness of Joseph must be the result of divinity. In all of Egypt, there was no one like Joseph. And because of his character, his gift, and his faith, Joseph reached the pinnacle of political power in Egypt. It was not their sermons or their proselytizing that revealed God to the Egyptians. It was his character.

DANIEL AND THE THREE HEBREW BOYS[281]

The story of Shadrach, Meshach, and Abednego is possibly one of the most familiar stories from the Old Testament. Their story intertwines with the story of Daniel because they were literally occurring at the same time. These four young men found themselves captive in the King's palace. On four separate occasions, their faith and their character was tested. Each time they maintained their faith and their character, it led not only to promotion but to the full recognition of our God by a pagan political system.

Often times, the Old-Testament retells the same story in different settings and with different characters in order to convey a significant point.[282] Daniel's story is an example of this type of retelling. It is, perhaps, the most significant because we see that on two different occasions and underneath two different pagan regimes, Daniel's character elevated him to cabinet level positions. Daniel's integrity and faith also led the different kings to the knowledge of God. It is as if God was saying, "In case you missed it the first time, this is an instant-replay so that you can clearly understand how believers should engage in a secular political system."

MORAL OF THE STORY

In none of these stories do we see the believer attempting to take over the political structure in order to install a theocracy. None of these men attempted to force their beliefs on anyone else in the foreign kingdoms or condemned those that did not believe as they did; instead, they personally lived up to the standards dictated by their faith. Their victories were less about pointing out what the secular nation was doing wrong and more about being true to their beliefs, even in a secular nation.

Sermons did not lead them to the top of the political structure. It was their character and their God-given abilities. Condemnation of others did not lead the secular nations to God. It was the result of God reveling himself through their faith in the face of great adversity.

Surely Joseph, Daniel, Shadrach, Meshach, and Abednego saw behaviors and lifestyles that were not in line with what they knew about God. Nevertheless, these men changed the course of those secular nations with their character and their personal integrity in the face of great temptation and tribulation.

We need Christian men and women whose personal character, integrity, and faith lift up the essence of Christ. This is the drawing force that will bring all men unto Him. This is what will lead them to the top of our political system. This is what the world is earnestly waiting to see: the character of Christ, not just the rhetoric of religion. When people who do not believe in God see how far the character of Christ can take true Christians in politics, they will have to respond like Nebuchadnezzar:

> Blessed be the God of Shadrach, Meshach, and Abednego...because there is no other God that can deliver [like this].—Daniel 3:28-29 (KJV)

We would be wise as Christians to learn that we can do far more for the Kingdom of God by being the best Christians we can be rather than attempting to use legislation to force others to abide by our rules.

Afterword

I am an eighties baby. My generation grew up with the presidential portrait of Ronald Reagan hanging on the walls of our elementary school classrooms. His face was amiable, yet slightly worn from the many years that he had journeyed. In many ways, Reagan was like a distant member of the family whose name always found its way into the conversations around our dinner table.

My first detailed memory as a child was of watching the Space Shuttle Challenger takeoff on its way into space. I was home sitting next to a laundry basket and entirely too close to the television. I don't recall why I was at home instead of in school that day. Perhaps the cold weather of January had gotten to me. My mother was in the kitchen while my brother and sisters were still in school. Although we were not all together, we all watched the events unfolding live on television. We all saw an American tragedy occur right before our eyes. Like most five-year olds, I was unable to grasp the magnitude of what was going on. All I could tell was that something terrible had happened to all of us: not just to my family, but to every American family.

Later that day, and for the first time, the man whose picture hung in my classroom spoke directly to me. Just as he predicted, I didn't understand his words right then. But later in life as I watched a recording of his speech online, I was instantly transformed into the child sitting too close to the television, playing with his mother's laundry basket, and trying to understand what he saw as our Challenger and her seven

American heroes "slipped the surly bonds of earth, and touched the face of God."[283]

This was the generation I was born into. Nothing before it existed beyond what was written in our social studies books. Likewise, there was no political existence for our generation prior to the Reagan Administration. All we have known, all of our lives, is the political reality that we were born into. And to that end, I, like most of my generation, never knew that there was a time before this in which it wasn't a foregone conclusion that because I was Christian, I must also be a Republican. We were born into a political era in which it seemed only right that a good Christian would also be Republican because their party was the party with religious values.

I am the son of black Baptist preacher. I was born into a uniquely different Christian experience than believers of a different hue. My knowledge of God not only included long, intoned recitations of Calvary and the Resurrection, but also included local churches coming together to boycott several businesses in Brookhaven, Mississippi, that had not completely gotten Jim Crow out of their system. Yes, the sermons I heard were of the saving grace of Jesus Christ, but also of the liberating power of a savior who would one day bring justice for all of his children—including us. Although limited in scope, this was the religious reality that I was born into. This was the scope of my political and religious realities.

And so, for the last thirty-plus years, I've grown up with an agonizing dissonance in my brain. On the one hand, I saw an increasing amount of conflation between the Republican Party and Christianity. On the other hand, my experience of God taught me that He could not be entirely pleased with the GOP. They were incapable of being righteous enough to be deemed the "Party of Christ." I couldn't yet understand it as I grappled with it over the years. I tried to resolve the tension on my own but to no avail. What I had was a nagging suspicion that I was unable to verbalize until, finally, He gave me the words I had been searching for all my life: God is not a Republican.

As frivolous and obvious as this may be to some, for those like me, born into a generation in which Christianity is constantly and erroneously equated with Republicanism, or for those struggling with the nuances of their faith and their politics, this Word from God was like manna. God is not a Republican nor is He a Democrat. God is not an American, and theologically speaking, God is not even a "he." God is more. The creator of the known universe is more than any of us could ever imagine, and far more than religion could ever confine. Likewise, the Kingdom of God is greater than any man-made socio-political construct. The true Kingdom is incompatible with any political system including American politics.

I am afraid that we mixed God with politics for so long that, like my entire generation, most people can't recall a time when Christianity wasn't mistaken for Republicanism and Republicanism for Christianity. Although this confusion has been beneficial for the GOP, helping to elect one Republican candidate after another, I believe it has been detrimental to the cause of Christ. Instead of drawing all men unto him, many of the people who need to be reached with the message of Christ have turned away because of the politics of our faith.[284]

The evidence of this is around us every day. I will never forget going to a local Christian bookstore to buy a Bible to have inscribed for my mother-in-law as a gift for staying with us after we had our son. The very first book I saw as I walked in wasn't a Bible or a biblical study guide. The most prominent book on display in the Christian Bookstore was Sarah Palin's latest work, *American by Heart: Reflections on Family, Faith, and Flag*. Certainly, the bookstore understood that a large portion of their clientele would be interested in buying this product. This was effective marketing, but this also was indicative of the seamless conflation between the Republican politics and Christianity. No Christian should feel compelled to vote with either particular party because neither party is capable of representing Christ. It is possible that the title of this also came from the frustration I felt that day in the Christian bookstore.

Revelations on "God's Politics"

1980 to 1990 was a great decade to be a kid. Special effects were just coming of age in the movies. Saturday morning cartoons looked more like the comic page in the newspaper than graphic novels and anime. Sunday television was filled with movies that are now considered classics like Goonies, Star Wars, and Indiana Jones. Admittedly, I rarely got the chance to stay home on a Sunday. Whenever we didn't go to church, our mother would find sanctuary in her room and said the words we loved to hear: "Don't call me. I won't call you."

What I remember most about watching TV in the 80s was the televangelist our father turned on every Sunday as we got ready to go to church: D. James Kennedy. We watched Dr. Kennedy so much that growing up that we were able to recite his mailing address as though it was our own. Even to this day my siblings and I can quote from memory:

James Kennedy, Box 40, Ft. Lauderdale, FL, 33302.

Later in life we would move from Mississippi to Pompano Beach, Florida. It was only about five miles away from Coral Ridge Presbyterian Church. Passing by that towering building on occasion always took us back to those days we grew up looking at the towering steeple through the television.

It was while living in Florida that I discovered and read Dr. Kennedy's book on politics. By that time, I had already begun forming my own political opinions and was somewhat aware of his positions because of his high profile. What I wasn't aware of was the extent to which he allowed his great intellectual

Afterword

prowess to be put aside in order to conform to Republican ideology. Dr. Kennedy was a genius. His theological writings were astounding. Yet, his reasoning as to why Christians should adhere to the conservative political ideology was bereft of any great thoughts. This was not only a disappointment but also an eye opener. Many of our great pastors are involved with politics without careful consideration of the spiritual implications.

Revelations on Healthcare

Growing up the son of a preacher who pastored a small Baptist church in Mississippi, I had a unique understanding of what living without health insurance was like. The church wasn't big enough to offer any type of insurance or retirement. Thankfully, I was blessed to go through my entire youth without ever getting any sickness that required a hospital visit. And with the exception of a few bruised ribs from fights, somehow I made it through without breaking any bones.

What made my experience memorable was at the beginning of every school year when our homeroom teachers had us fill out the paperwork needed for school. Part of that paperwork included information on our family doctor. But seeing as my father was supporting six kids with no health insurance, we never had a family doctor. When I was old enough to fill out the forms myself, I asked my mother who I should put in for our doctor. She told me to write in, "Jesus." I am sure my mother did not expect me to write in "Jesus," as my doctor, but I'm certain there is a form in the Broward County School System that has Jesus listed as my family doctor. Truthfully, He had to be our doctor considering my parents were able to raise six of us without any health insurance; that in itself is a miracle.

My first full-time job as an adult was as the music director at a large church in Palm Beach County, Florida. The pay was sufficient for me to live on my own and pay my way through school. Even though the ministry was large, and although I was a full-time employee, the job did not offer any health insurance. Like my father before me, I had to manage without any type of healthcare. Thankfully, I didn't have the responsibility of a family at the time.

One night I started experiencing unbearable chest pains. After about ten minutes of the pain, I ruled out a heart attack because I was still alive. My friends insisted that I go to the hospital. Because I knew that I didn't have any insurance, I refused. After dealing with the pain that kept me awake from 6:00 PM to 7:00 AM I decided to give in and go. My roommate drove me to the emergency room.

As I filled out the forms in the hospital and came to the line requesting the name of my primary-care physician, I couldn't help but reminisce on how things had not changed much since I was little. I still had no insurance and no family doctor. I smiled, and considered writing in "Jesus" as my doctor like I had years before.

I'm grateful that my diagnosis was only a bad case of acid reflux. They told me take Pepcid AC® in order to keep the symptoms down. Unfortunately, that diagnosis cost me $6,000 when a family doctor could have given me the same information for a tenth of the price.

This Book

This book is the result of years of conflicting thoughts and cognitive dissonance. I heard the religious words of politicians and saw the mobilization of pastors. But because of my personal experience with God, I felt the emptiness of the words Republican politicians gave. Although I agreed with some of the Republican platforms, it was difficult for me to agree with the spirit behind their social policies. I found them to be both constitutionally and biblically wrong.

What was most disturbing to me was to see the blind devotion many Christians had for the party even though the

Afterword

party had accomplished little to nothing for the Christian cause. What was worse was when I saw how detrimental the coalition has been for the cause of Christ. So many people turn away from the Faith; not because they don't want to accept Christ but, rather, because they refuse to accept the politics that we have attached to Him.

I've been asked whether this is a political book about religion or a religious book about politics. My favorite answer is both. For me, it is both a political book which seeks to biblically refute the religious objections to certain policies, and a political book that seeks to expose the effects politics has had our faith. Each chapter tackles both facets. Each chapter deals with a particular political issue and offers a biblical argument as to why Christians should or should not oppose it. At the same time, each chapter deals with how the Republican Party has craftily positioned itself to benefit from the Christian vote while never actually delivering on the issues we often vote for

Part of me believes this book will be rejected because of the strength of the Evangelical-Republican coalition. However, the idealistic part of me believes that a person who is sincere about their faith and love for Christ will be able to see past the politics that divide us long enough to at least consider that the Evangelical-Republican coalition is not what we have told it was.

We are all free to vote for whatever candidates we feel will do the job we want done. With this in mind, I am not trying to change how evangelicals vote. My goal is to destroy the lingering notion that, because Republicans talk in religious terms, promote family values, and oppose abortion, we as Christians have a spiritual obligation to vote with them. And if this notion persists, then we must come to terms with the utter failure of the Republican Party to deliver a true victory for any of the causes from which they earned our votes.

Notes

Introduction Notes

[1] Prior to the mobilization of this faithful voting bloc in the 1980 election cycle, Republicans and Conservatives were unable to gain a majority in both houses of congress for thirty-two years—an entire generation. Although the GOP was effective in electing moderate Republicans to the White House, they were completely unsuccessful electing conservatives prior to Ronald Reagan. All of this changed as the GOP realized what it was missing from its platform: values-voters.

[2] Even today, the strength of the Christian voting bloc remains a force to be reckoned with. In the mid-term elections of 2010, it was the Christian Evangelical vote that helped sweep the Republican Party back into power across the nation.

[3] Christianity is from the Greek word Χριστιανός which translates as "follower of Christ"

Prologue Notes

[4] The historical account throughout this prologue was derived by triangulating five sources: William Martin's *With God on our Side;* Sarah Diamond's *Spiritual Warfare: The Politics of the Christian Right*, and *Facing the Wrath: Confronting the Right in Dangerous Times*; Julia Anderson's *Mr. Conservative: Goldwater on Goldwater*; and the documentary version of Martin's book, *With God on Our Side*. These sources have been invaluable in piecing together the rise of the Religious Right in America. Martin and Diamond, in particular, should be considered eminent scholars on the history of the Religious Right.

[5] This phrase is taken directly from James Robison as quoted in *With God on Our Side*, p.204. (Martin 1996)

[6] (Martin 1996, 214-215)

[7] (Anderson 2006)

[8] (Martin 1996, 208)

[9] (Ibid, 217)

[10] Many modern politicians can learn from Reagan's wisdom in this regard.

[11] (Diamond, Spiritual Warfare: The Politics of the Christian Right 1989, 56)

[12] (Carter 2011)

[13] (Skaggs, Van Talyor and Pomeroy 2004)

Notes

14 Ibid
15 See (Martin 1996, 208)
16 See the Biblical story of Joseph. Book of Genesis chapter 37
17 (Martin 1996, 214)
18 Decided by the Supreme Court January 22, 1973
19 Supreme Court Decisions in 1962, 1963, and 1971 each led to the "secularization" of school activity
20 An alternative viewpoint of the rise of the Religious Right is offered by Randall Balmer in his book, *Thy Kingdom Come* (Balmer 2006). Balmer references Paul Weyrich's comments at a conservative conference at which he suggests that the mobilization of the Religious Right was the result of opposition to the IRS threatening Bob Jones University tax-exempt status because of the school's discriminatory practices. This would suggest that the Religious Right was and the Evangelical Coalition was initially motivated in opposition to segregation. This contention is opposed by many in evangelical circles.
21 (Diamond, Spiritual Warfare: The Politics of the Christian Right 1989, 55)
22 (Martin 1996, 204)
23 (Martin 1996, 99)
24 (ibid, 1996, p. 99)
25 (ibid, 1996, 99)
26 (Skaggs, Van Talyor and Pomeroy 2004)
27 (ibid, 2004)
28 (ibid, 2004)
29 There are several accounts of this meeting. Each account has different attendees. The names listed here are the names shared by each source.
30 (Skaggs, Van Talyor and Pomeroy 2004)
31 (Diamond, Spiritual Warfare: The Politics of the Christian Right 1989, 60), (Diamond, Roads to Dominion: Right-Wing Movements and Political Power in the United States 1995, 174) and (Martin 1996, 200)
32 (Skaggs, Van Talyor and Pomeroy 2004)
33 (Diamond, Roads to Dominion: Right-Wing Movements and Political Power in the United States 1995)
34 As quoted by Jerry Falwell in the documentary, *With God on our Side*, (Skaggs, Van Talyor and Pomeroy 2004)
35 Sixty-Six percent of white Baptists voted for Carter in 1976. Sixty-four percent voted for Reagan four years later.
36 Isaiah 53:6
37 Today a presidential candidate would have to distance himself from such rhetoric.

Notes

38 (Skaggs, Van Talyor and Pomeroy 2004)

Chapter 1 Notes

39 Scripture quotations marked (NIV) are taken from the Holy Bible, New International Version® (International Bible Society 1973, 1978, 1984)
40 See Deuteronomy 30:11-19
41 While our nation is not a direct democracy, consensus among the few hundred representatives we have elected in our republic has proven to be cripplingly difficult.
42 "If a nation expects to be ignorant and free, in a state of civilization, it expects what never was and never will be." (Jefferson, Full text of "The Writings of Thomas Jefferson" 1899)

Chapter 2 Notes

43 (Kennedy and Newcombe 2008)
44 (Ibid, 2008, p. 9)
45 Scripture quotations marked (ESV) are from (Crossway Bibles 2001)
46 (Christian Answers Action 2006)
47 Ibid, 2006, p. 3
48 Ibid, 2006, pp. 6-8
49 Ibid, 2006, p. 15
50 Ibid, 2006, p. 16
51 (Kennedy and Newcombe 2008)
52 Scripture quotations marked (KJV) are from the King James Bible
53 See 1 John 5:16
54 (Crossway Bibles 2001)
55 For those who reference the scripture labeling homosexuality an "abomination," please read Proverbs 6:16-19
56 Acts 17:6
57 (Skaggs, Van Talyor and Pomeroy 2004)
58 Ibid, 2004
59 (Diamond, Spiritual Warfare: The Politics of the Christian Right 1989, 64), (Diamond, Roads to Dominion: Right-Wing Movements and Political Power in the United States 1995, 214), (Anderson 2006), (Martin 1996, 227-229)
60 (Anderson 2006)
61 In response, Conservative leader Barry Goldwater replied: "All good Christians should kick Jerry Falwell in the ass." (Anderson 2006)

Notes

[62] (Diamond, Spiritual Warfare: The Politics of the Christian Right 1989, 72), (Skaggs, Van Talyor and Pomeroy 2004)
[63] (Diamond, Spiritual Warfare: The Politics of the Christian Right 1989, 75),
[64] (Skaggs, Van Talyor and Pomeroy 2004), (Martin 1996, 314-315)
[65] (Skaggs, Van Talyor and Pomeroy 2004)
[66] (Rutenberg 2006)
[67] (Stout 2004)
[68] Scripture quotations marked (KJV) are from the King James Bible
[69] (Skaggs, Van Talyor and Pomeroy 2004)
[70] (NBC Universal Television Distribution 2006)
[71] See Joshua 24:15
[72] Calvinists, and other believers in predestination, disagree with assertion. Adherents of the Calvinist tradition believe in predestination. This simply means that those of us that are saved were already chosen by God to be saved. In this, they believe that God's grace was irresistible and, in fact, we could not choose Him because we had no ability to resist Him. This is a valid theological debate that continues today. See Calvinism vs. Arminianism.
[73] Thirteenth century Theologian and Philosopher
[74] (Koritansky 2007)
[75] "He who expects to be made pure without any effort of his own, will never become pure; and he who ever becomes holy will become so in consequence of strenuous efforts to resist the evil of his own heart, and to become like God." (Barnes 1847)

Chapter 3 Notes

[76] Between 1973 and 2008 over 50 million legal abortions were performed. (Guttmacher Institute 2011)
[77] One contradiction that I have yet to resolve is how enlightening Christ is, yet how unbelievably narrow-minded religious views can be.
[78] Justices Brennan and Stewart were appointed by President Eisenhower. Justices Berger, Blackmun, Powell, and Rehnquist were each appointed by President Nixon.
[79] Justice White, one of the two dissenters on Roe v. Wade, was appointed by President Kennedy.
[80] (Guttmacher Institute 2011)
[81] Ibid
[82] If you consider human nature in its most noble and honorable sense, this assertion may seem absurd. However, considering the true nature of politics and power, this is a strategic consideration

Notes

that is benefited by the fact that the GOP is very likely unable to achieve the ultimate goal of the pro-life movement: a reversal of Roe v. Wade. And so, abortion is a useful protracted battle that will continuously move pro-lifers to the polls without any substantive victories on their behalf.

[83] (Strickland 2011)
[84] (Guttmacher Institute 2011)
[85] Notwithstanding the religious debate, contraception is proven to reduce the number of abortions.
[86] See Joshua 24:15 and Deuteronomy 30:19
[87] See Chapter 3: Oppressive Freedom
[88] Thirty-seven percent identify as Protestant. Twenty-eight percent identify as Catholic. (Guttmacher Institute 2011)
[89] No matter what you believe regarding homosexuality—whether you believe it to be a sin, not a sin, a greater sin, or an equal sin—we all must agree that what two consenting adults choose to do can never be placed in the same category as an adult sexually assaulting a child. They are not comparable and I only mention them in the same paragraph to demonstrate the hypocrisy that plagues our churches, both Protestant and Catholic.
[90] (The Barna Group, Ltd 2008)
[91] (Wind 2005)
[92] My usage of absolutism is not in reference to the philosophical meaning of absolutes; but, rather, in reference to the uncompromising positions that we often take up when we believe that we are absolutely right and those we disagree with are absolutely wrong.

Chapter 4 Notes

[93] Taking any position to its logical extreme always produces an absurdity. This position does not mean that people can marry their beloved pets, appliances, and/or underage children even if their religion endorses it. In this detail we can be assured that the government will always have a role even in the religious definition of marriage.
[94] (Shah 2004)
[95] (104th Congress 1996)
[96] Clinton would later regret signing this law and call for its repeal.
[97] (Williams 2012)
[98] See Romans 3:23
[99] (International Bible Society 1973, 1978, 1984)

Notes

Chapter 5 Notes

[100] My use of Obamacare is not meant to be derogatory. Indeed, I believe the term will one day be a lasting monument to the president that fought to make healthcare accessible for all Americans.
[101] (CNN 2011)
[102] The question posed was a loaded question. Any direct answer would have been detrimental to Congressman Paul's campaign. Dr. Paul redirected the question with an answer on "liberty."
[103] (CNN 2011)
[104] The three "yeah(s)" and the audience laughter is not recorded in the CNN transcript of the Republican debate. It can be viewed at http://www.youtube.com/watch?v=2OLqy__eAH4
[105] (CNN 2011)
[106] The Affordable Care Act, Obamacare, is in many ways modeled after a Republican policy plan.
[107] We have entered into an era in which "Redistribution" is equated with "Socialism" and "Communism," and consequently is looked upon with suspicion and contempt.
[108] (Berwick 2011)
[109] (Holan 2012)
[110] (Memoli 2010)
[111] See the 180 degree Republican turnaround on the Dream Act and the Individual mandate; both of which were originally Republican concepts.
[112] See the Afterword for more details
[113] Particularly in regards to the Affordable Care Act, the debate was often framed as "Why should our tax dollars go to support the poor? We should be able to decide when we want to give to the poor." The irony of this is that the legislation was aimed at helping the middle class. The poor already have Medicaid.
[114] (Candisky 2010)
[115] (Donohue 2009)
[116] (YouTube 2009)

Chapter 6 Notes

[117] All of the statistics in this paragraph were gathered from ((Pew Research Center 2009)
[118] (Pew Research Center 2011)
[119] Eighty-eight percent voted for John Kerry in 2004 while ninety-five percent voted for Barack Obama in 2008. On average, seventy-

Notes

six percent identify themselves as Democratic. (Pew Research Center 2009)

[120] (Cain 2011)
[121] (Jackson 2008)
[122] Ibid
[123] Dixiecrats is the pseudonym used for Southern Democrats. The historical political party dissolved in 1948. Electoral Maps indicate that the southern states that had previously voted with the Democratic Party in 1960 voted with the Republican Party in 1964. See (Carmine and Stimson 1989)
[124] (Kuhn 2009), (Jackson 2008)
[125] (Southern Poverty Law Center 2009)
[126] (Boyd 1970)
[127] (Hays 2003, 23), (Krugman, The Conscience of a Liberal 2007)
[128] (CBS News 2011)
[129] It is often in the poorest neighborhoods that parents awaken before their children so they can catch public transportation and make it to work by 6:00 AM for minimum wage. Migrant workers, and often undocumented workers, toil from dawn until dusk for minimum wage or less. Gingrich's comments were illogical and counterfactual.
[130] (Elliot 2012)
[131] Politifact® verified that more Americans are on food stamps today than since its inception in 1969. However, they rated this statement as "half true" since the growth in food stamp recipients began during the Bush Administration. (Politifact.com 2011)
[132] (Hays 2003, 23)
[133] (Fox News 2012)
[134] (Killough 2012)
[135] Gingrich did not simply play to the latent "racism" of the South. He also succeeded because he was seen to be attacking the liberally "biased" media which is always portrayed as an enemy of the Republican Party.
[136] (Fox News 2012)
[137] (Meyers 2012)
[138] For the polls prior to the debate see (Mason 2012), and for the results of the primary see (New York Times 2012)
[139] (Matthews, MSNBC Transcripts 1-18-2012 2012)
[140] (Matthews, MSNBC Transcripts 1-17-2012 2012)
[141] (Di Fino 2012)
[142] (Harris-Perry 2007)
[143] Harris-Perry quotes William Jones (Harris-Perry 2007)
[144] Ibid
[145] (Harris-Perry 2007)

Notes

146 (Harris-Lacewell 2007, 158)
147 (Harris-Perry 2007)
148 (Pew Research Center 2009) The research question was specifically asking about a government large enough to provide resources. The implication in the text is based on federal government intervention that potentially conflicts with states' rights.
149 (Norquist 2001)
150 (Pew Research Center 2012)
151 (Pew Research Center 2007)
152 (Pew Research Center 2012)
153 (Pew Research Center 2007)

Section 2 Introduction Notes

154 These policies are synthesized from multiple public references of various Republican candidates, conservative advocates, and conservative political/economic pundits.
155 Admittedly, this is an oversimplification of Republican economic policies. Nevertheless, each of their policies can be derived from these six main points.

156 This assertion is based on the preferential tax treatment of income from capital gains versus labor.
157 See 2 Thessalonians 3:10

Chapter 7 Notes

158 (Jefferson 1782)
159 (Catechism of the Catholic Church, 1943-1948)
160 ibid
161 (NPR/Kaiser/Kennedy School 2001)
162 (Zinn 1989, 863)
163 Corporate welfare comes in many forms including tax subsidies. Social welfare also comes in many forms including Social Security, Medicare and Medicaid. The General Welfare is a term taken from the Preamble of the Constitution and is generally interpreted to mean our nation's infrastructure: roads, highways, bridges, and the postal service.

Chapter 8 Notes

164 (Skaggs, Van Talyor and Pomeroy 2004)

Notes

[165] Id is defined in Oxford dictionary as: "the part of the mind in which innate instinctive impulses and primary processes are manifest."

[166] (Mumford 1944, 1972, 1972, 182)

[167] It is important to note that Mumford does not consider Adam Smith's The Wealth of Nations to be the beginning of capitalism. He looks at the two centuries before Smith and considers that time to be the period of formation. From his perspective, capitalism grew into a coherent theory and faced opposition for several centuries prior to Smith's work.

[168] (Guzik 2004)

[169] (Guzik 2004)

[170] These scriptures have been comprehensively compiled and made available courtesy of (Tentmaker.com 2012)

[171] With this scripture we have to answer the question of "Who is our brother or sister?" While this scripture may be dismissed as referring to immediate family, it coincides with so many other scriptures that clearly express God's rejection of His children requiring interest of one another.

[172] (Thomas Nelson, Inc. 2001)

[173] See (Kennedy and Newcombe 2008, 102-103)

[174] Scriptures such as Leviticus 25:35-38, Matthew 19:16-24, Matthew 25:31-46, Luke 1:49-53, John 2:14-16, and Acts 4:32 each contributed to the birth of Christian Communism and Christian Socialism. Christian Communism never gained any significant ground in the larger Christian community. In fact the Christian Communist work, Le vrai Christianisme suivant Jesus-Christ (The Real Christianity According to Jesus Christ), by nineteenth century French theologian and philosopher, Étienne Cabet, was never translated into English.

[175] See Colossians 3:22-24

[176] See (Creationists.org 2012)

[177] (E. Smith 2011)

[178] (King 1971, 376)

Chapter 9 Notes

[179] (Blackburn 2008)

[180] Not if free markets is defined as zero governmental and private influence.

[181] Capitalism is not by nature necessarily zero-sum.

[182] These two points are intrinsic to capitalism. These are two of the many forces that contribute to the institutionalization of poverty and wealth disparity.

Notes

183 The title of this section is taken from Winston Churchill's famous quote regarding capitalism and socialism. See (Churchill 1945)
184 (A. Smith, Wealth of Nations 1776)
185 Ibid
186 (A. Smith 1776)
187 The "Kids for Cash" judicial scandal is what occurred in Luzerne County, Pennsylvania. Two juvenile court judges were receiving kickbacks from a for-profit juvenile facility in exchange for convictions.
188 (Doomen 2005)
189 Both men were convicted of massive ponzi schemes.
190 (Huffington Post 2011)
191 This analogy can be furthered by introducing teenage gangs into the room full of children. These gangs would represent conglomerates, oligopolies, and multinational corporations.
192 Federalist Paper #51 (Madison, The Federalist No. 51 1788)
193 If one defines the free market as having no undue influence from the government or powerful private entities and individuals.
194 (Sumner 1883, 1974, 18-19)
195 See (Jilani 2010) for example.
196 (A. Smith 1776)
197 See the Gospel of Luke 21:1-4
198 The self-interest of the butcher and the baker Adam Smith wrote about in Wealth of Nations. (A. Smith, Wealth of Nations 1776)
199 This is why we should be wary of anyone crusading to make government so small that you can drown it in a bathtub.

Chapter 10 Notes

200 (Spurgeon 1859, 403)
201 (Barlcay 1957, 1975, 2001, 319)
202 (Hobbes 1651)
203 (Olson 1993)
204 Trickle-Down Economic Theory supports tax breaks for businesses, "job creators" and the wealthiest among us. The idea behind this theory is that this group would reinvest these funds and create more jobs and economic growth. Wealth would then "trickle-down" to all citizens.
205 (Skaggs, Van Talyor and Pomeroy 2004)
206 (Sahadi 2010)
207 Tax rates increased from 28% underneath Reagan, George H.W. Bush, and Bill Clinton.

Notes

[208] (National Taxpayers Union 2009)
[209] Government expenditures increased during this period particularly in defense spending. See (Sahadi 2010)
[210] (Internal Revenue Service 2012)
[211] This was true with both the Reagan (Deseret News 1989) and Bush Tax Cuts (Economic Policy Institute 2003)
[212] This is evident by the slow growth in employment under the Bush tax cuts. (PolitiFact.com 2011)
[213] (CBS 2011)
[214] (Sawhill 2008)

Chapter 11 Notes

[215] (Isaacs 2008)
[216] (Solon 1992)
[217] (Isaacs 2008)
[218] (Solon 1992, 405)
[219] (Fukuyama 1992, 2006, 290)
[220] It is important to make the distinction between the socialist economic system and socialist styled policies. The economic system seeks to divide all wealth evenly among citizens. Socialist style policies redistribute wealth through taxation for the purposes of providing a benefit to the entire nation or a specific group. Our military, infrastructure, and education are examples of socialist style policies in that they collect taxes, redistribute to another segment, and provide a benefit for society.
[221] (Churchill 1945)
[222] See (Haskins, Isaacs and Sawhill 2008), (Isaacs 2008), and (Solon 1992)
[223] (A. Smith 1776)
[224] Ibid
[225] (A. Smith, Of the Revenue of the Sovereign or Commonwealth 1776)

Chapter 12 Notes

[226] (Falwell 2004)
[227] Jerry Falwell made many tremendous contributions to the Body of Christ. His best legacy will always be the work he did at Thomas Road Baptist Church and Liberty University.
[228] (Liberty University 2011)
[229] Ibid
[230] See Luke 4:18

Notes

[231] (The Lockman Foundation 1954, 1958, 1962, 1964, 1965, 1987)
[232] (Republican National Committee 2010)
[233] an unreasonable fear of foreigners or strangers or of that which is foreign or strange
[234] As evident by Rick Perry's decline in the polls after he defended Texas' version of the Dream Act
[235] See (Exline, et al. 2011)
[236] (CBS 2011)
[237] (Coulter, Ann Coulter wants Jews "to be perfected" 2007)
[238] (Coulter 2011)
[239] (CBS News 2011)
[240] (ABC News 2012)
[241] (CNN 2011) The three "yeah(s)" and the audience laughter is not recorded in the transcript; however, they can be heard in the video at http://www.youtube.com/watch?v=2OLqy__eAH4

Chapter 13 Notes

[242] (Clausewitz 1873)
[243] (Martin 1996, 99)
[244] (CBS News 2011)
[245] (Innocence Project)
[246] (Southern Baptist Convention 2000)
[247] See Romans 6:23

Chapter 14 Notes

[248] See (Massa 1997) for a detailed analysis of the speech and the circumstances surrounding the speech.
[249] (J. F. Kennedy 1960)
[250] (Pew Research 2010)
[251] The very foundation of our salvation is based on our confession of faith. See Romans 10:9
[252] (Katchen 2012)
[253] (Obama 2012)
[254] See the book of Matthew chapter 4
[255] (Helderman 2012)
[256] Eisegetical interpretations are interpretations of scripture that make the verse say more than what it explicitly says.
[257] Spurgeon is considered to be one of the greatest theological minds in Christianity.
[258] This tirade of terms was popular during the healthcare debate between 2009 and 2010.

[259] (Roach 2011)
[260] (Jeffress 2012)
[261] Ibid
[262] (Huffington Post 2009)
[263] President Obama has clearly stated that he is not "pro-abortion."
[264] Idolatry – extreme admiration, love, or reverence for something or someone. Oxford Dictionaries (Oxford 2012)
[265] At which point we will be thankful for religious freedom and the separation of church and state.
[266] (Newell 1994, 483)

Chapter 15 Notes

[267] (Washington 1789)
[268] (Washington 1792)
[269] **(Madison 1785, #1)**

[270] This quote is the closest to an endorsement of faith from James Madison. In context, he is stating that every man's faith is subject to his personal beliefs; therefore, it cannot be forced.
[271] (Madison 1785, #8)
[272] (Monticello)
[273] (Jefferson, Notes on the State of Virginia 1781)
[274] (Adams 1798)
[275] This quote is generally attributed to John Adams.
[276] (Franklin 1728)
[277] (New York Historical Society 1849, 142)

Chapter 16 Notes

[278] See Galatians 5:22-23
[279] See Philippians 2:12
[280] Joseph's political experience in Egypt can be found in the Book of Genesis, chapters 39-41
[281] For those not familiar with these stories, read the Book of Daniel chapters 1-6.
[282] (Gunn and Fewell 1993)

Afterword Notes

[283] Taken from Reagan's speech following the Challenger disaster.
[284] See John 12:32

Bibliography

104th Congress. "GPO.gov." September 21, 1996. http://frwebgate.access.gpo.gov/cgi-bin/getdoc.cgi?dbname=104_cong_public_laws&docid=f:publ19 9.104 (accessed March 2, 2012).

ABC News. *Audience Boos Gay Soldier at GOP Debate.* Ferbuary 23, 2012. http://abcnews.go.com/Primetime/video/audience-boos-gay-soldier-gop-debate-15776133 (accessed March 3, 2012).

Adams, John. *Proclamation 8 - Recommending a National Day of Humiliation, Fasting, and Prayer.* March 23, 1798. http://www.presidency.ucsb.edu/ws/index.php?pid=65661#a xzz1sJlvVW3s (accessed March 2012).

Aldrich, John H. "Why Parties?" In *Principles and Practice of American Politics: Classic and Contemporary Readings*, edited by Samuel Kernell and Steven S Smith, 587-599. Washington D.C.: CQ Press, 2010.

Mr. Conservative: Goldwater on Goldwater. Directed by Julie Anderson. Produced by Sweat Pea Films. 2006.

Balmer, Randall. *Thy Kingdom Come: An Evangelical's Lament.* New York: Basic Books, 2006.

Barlcay, William. *The New Daily Study Bible.* Louisville: Westminster John Knox Press, 1957, 1975, 2001.

Barnes, Albert. *Notes, Explanatory and Practical on the Second Epistle to the Corinthians adn the Epistle to the Galations.* New York: Harper & Brothers, 1847.

Berg, Delvin R. *Lyndon B. Johnson Online Museum.* 2008. http://www.lyndonbjohnson.org/Biography.html (accessed November 2011).

Berwick, Donald, interview by Tom Ashbrook. "Former Medicare Chief Donald Berwick Speaks." *On Point*. National Public Radio. December 6, 2011.

Blackburn, Simon. *The Oxford Dictionary of Philosophy*. Oxford: Oxford University Press, 2008.

Blake, Aaron. *The Washington Post*. 2011. http://www.washingtonpost.com/blogs/the-fix/post/mitt-romney-establishment-candidate/2011/12/19/gIQAB2Yi4O_blog.html (accessed February 12, 2012).

Boyd, James. "New York Times." May 17, 1970. http://www.nytimes.com/packages/html/books/phillips-southern.pdf (accessed March 1, 2012).

Cain, Herman, interview by Wolf Blitzer. "Interview With GOP Presidential Candidate Herman Cain." *The Situation Room*. CNN. CNN. September 28, 2011.

With God on Our Side. Directed by David Van Talyor, Ali Pomeroy Calvin Skaggs. Produced by Lumiere Productions, Inc. 2004.

Candisky, Catherine. *The Columbus Dispatch*. 2010. http://www.dispatch.com/content/stories/local/2010/03/19/angry-protesters-warp-focus-of-debate.html (accessed September 2011).

Carmine, Edward, and James Stimson. *Issue Evolution: Race and the Transformation of American Politics*. Princeton: Princeton University Press, 1989.

Carter, Jimmy, interview by Rachel Maddow. "The Rachel Maddow Show." *The Rachel Maddow Show*. MSNBC. September 16, 2011.

Catechism of the Catholic Church. "Catechism of the Catholic Church." *Vatican*.

Bibliography

http://www.vatican.va/archive/ccc_css/archive/catechism/p3s1c2a3.htm (accessed April 6, 2012).

CBS. *The Pledge: Grover Norquist's hold on the GOP.* November 20, 2011. http://www.cbsnews.com/8301-18560_162-57327816/the-pledge-grover-norquists-hold-on-the-gop/ (accessed March 3, 2012).

CBS News. *CBSNews.Com.* 2011. http://www.cbsnews.com/video/watch/?id=7390203n (accessed February 2012).

—. *Rick Perry Defends Texas Death Penalty Record.* September 7, 2011. http://www.cbsnews.com/video/watch/?id=7380162n (accessed February 2012).

Christian Answers Action. *Voter's Guide for Serious Christians.* El Cajon: Christian Answers Action, 2006.

Churchill, Winston. "Demobilisation." *MillBankSystems.com.* October 22, 1945. http://hansard.millbanksystems.com/commons/1945/oct/22/demobilisation#column_1703 (accessed February 15, 2012).

Clausewitz, Carl Von. *On War.* Translated by Colonel J.J. Graham. London: N. Trübner, 1873.

CNN. "CNN Transcripts." September 12, 2011. http://archives.cnn.com/TRANSCRIPTS/1109/12/se.06.html (accessed December 2011).

Coulter, Ann, interview by Donny Deutsch. "Ann Coulter wants Jews "to be perfected"." *The Big Idea.* CNBC. October 7, 2007.

—. *Demonic: How the Liberal Mob is Endangering America.* New York: Crown Publishing, 2011.

Creationists.org. *Definition of Eisegesis.* 2012. http://creationists.org/definition-of-eisegesis.html (accessed March 2, 2012).

Crossway Bibles. *The Holy Bible, English Standard Version.* Crossway, a publishing ministry of Good News Publishers, 2001.

Deseret News. *Income Disparity Largest Since 1947.* December 31, 1989. http://www.deseretnews.com/article/79114/INCOME-DISPARITY-LARGEST-SINCE-1947.html (accessed April 4, 2012).

Di Fino, NNando. *Rep. Allen West Defends Newt Gingrich Against "Race Code" Accusations on Fox & Friends.* January 23, 2012. http://www.mediaite.com/tv/rep-allen-west-defends-newt-gingrich-against-race-code-accusations-on-fox-friends/ (accessed March 2, 2012).

Diamond, Sara. *Roads to Dominion: Right-Wing Movements and Political Power in the United States.* New York: The Guilford Press, 1995.

—. *Spiritual Warfare: The Politics of the Christian Right.* Boston: South End Press, 1989.

Donohue, Brian. *NJ.com.* 2009. http://www.nj.com/ledgerlive/index.ssf/2009/08/health_care_reform_town_hall_n.html (accessed September 15, 2011).

Doomen, Jasper. "Smith's Analysis of Human Actions." *Ethic@: an International Journal for Moral Philosophy*, December 2005: 111-122.

Eckholm, Erik. *The New York Times.* 2011. http://www.nytimes.com/2011/01/28/us/politics/28conservatives.html?pagewanted=all (accessed January 15, 2012).

Bibliography

Economic Policy Institute. "Economists' Statement Opposing the Bush Tax Cuts." *EPI.org*. 2003. http://www.epi.org/page/-/old/stmt/2003/statement_signed.pdf (accessed March 2012).

Elliot, Debbie. *'Food Stamp Presidet': Race Code, or Just Politics?* January 17, 2012. http://www.npr.org/2012/01/17/145312069/newts-food-stamp-president-racial-or-just-politics (accessed March 2, 2012).

Exline, Julie J., Crystal L. Park, Joshua M. Smyth, and Michael P. Carey. "Anger toward God: Social-cognitive predictors, prevalence, and links with adjustment to bereavement and cancer." *Journal of Personality and Social Psychology*, 2011: 129-148.

Falwell, Jerry. "Jerry Falwell: Ronald Reagan, My Hero." *NewsMax*. June 6, 2004. http://archive.newsmax.com/archives/articles/2004/6/5/182327.shtml (accessed March 3, 2012).

Fox News. *Gingrich: Blacks Should Demand Paychecks Not Food Stamps*. January 6, 2012. http://nation.foxnews.com/newt-gingrich/2012/01/06/newt-african-american-community-should-demand-pay-checks-and-not-be-satisfied-food-stamps (accessed March 2, 2012).

—. *Republican Presidential Debate*. January 16, 2012. http://www.foxnews.com/on-air/fox-news-debates/index.html#/v/1395835597001/gingrich-only-the-elites-despise-earning-money/?playlist_id=%201390070429001 (accessed March 2, 2012).

Franklin, Benjamin. "Articles of Belief and Acts of Religion." *Beliefnet.com*. November 20, 1728. http://www.beliefnet.com/resourcelib/docs/65/Articles_of_Belief_and_Acts_of_Religion_1.html (accessed April 3, 2012).

Fukuyama, Francis. *The End of History and the Last Man.* New York: Free Press, 1992, 2006.

Goldwater, Barry. *The Conscience of a Conservative.* New Jersey: Victor Publishing Company & Princeton University Press, 1960.

Greenblatt, Alan. *As U.S., Europe Hack at Budgets, Pensions Get Sliced.* 2011. http://www.npr.org/2011/12/01/143001121/in-u-s-and-europe-pensions-at-risk (accessed March 2, 2012).

Gunn, David, and Danna Fewell. *Narrative in the Hebrew Bible.* Oxford: Oxford University Press, 1993.

Guttmacher Institute. *Facts on Induced Abortion in the United States.* 2011. http://www.guttmacher.org/pubs/fb_induced_abortion.html#2 (accessed December 14, 2011).

Guzik, David. *Leviticus 25 - Special Sabbaths and Jubilees.* 2004. http://www.enduringword.com/commentaries/0325.htm (accessed March 28, 2012).

Harris-Lacewell, Melissa. "From Liberation to Mutual Fund: Political COnsequences of Differing Conceptions of Christ in the African American Church." In *From Pews to Polling Places*, by J. Matthew Wilson, 131-160. Washington D.C.: Georgetown University Press, 2007.

Harris-Perry, Melissa. "Righteous Politics: The Role of the Black Church in Contemporary Politics." *Cross Currents* 9, no. 1 (2007).

Haskins, Ron, Julia Isaacs, and Isabel Sawhill. *Getting Ahead or Losing Ground: Economic Mobility in America.* Economic Mobility Project, Washington, D.C.: The Brookings Institution, 2008.

Bibliography

Hays, Sharon. *Flat Broke with Children: Women in the Age of Welfare Reform.* New York: Oxford, 2003.

Helderman, Rosalind. *Rick Santorum's 'phony theology' criticism of Obama follows a familiar theme.* February 22, 2012. http://www.washingtonpost.com/politics/rick-santorums-phony-theology-criticism-of-obama-follows-a-familiar-theme/2012/02/21/gIQA3TIpTR_story.html (accessed March 2, 2012).

Hobbes, Thomas. *The Leviathan.* England: Andrew Crooke and William Cooke, 1651.

Holan, Angie. *Romneycare and Obamacare: Can you tell the Difference?* March 20, 2012. http://www.politifact.com/truth-o-meter/article/2012/mar/20/romneycare-and-obamacare-can-you-tell-difference/ (accessed March 28, 2012).

Huffington Post. *Obama Says He Prays 'All The Time' For Guidance.* September 23, 2009. http://www.huffingtonpost.com/2009/07/23/obama-says-he-prays-all-t_n_244029.html (accessed March 2, 2012).

—. *Wells Fargo Overdraft Lawsuits: Bank Ordered to Pay $203 Million in Fees Over 'Unfair' Charges.* 2011. http://www.huffingtonpost.com/2010/08/11/wells-fargo-overdraft-law_n_679178.html (accessed March 2, 2012).

Innocence Project. "Facts on Post-Conviction DNA Exonerations." *InnocenceProject.com.* http://www.innocenceproject.org/Content/Facts_on_PostConviction_DNA_Exonerations.php (accessed March 2012).

Internal Revenue Service. *Ten Things to Know About Capital Gains and Losses.* February 22, 2012. http://www.irs.gov/newsroom/article/0,,id=106799,00.html (accessed March 30, 2012).

International Bible Society. *The Holy Bible.* Zondervan Publishing House, 1973, 1978, 1984.

Isaacs, Julia. "Internationaal Comparisions of Economic Mobility." *Brookings Institution.* February 2008. http://www.brookings.edu/reports/2008/~/media/CFF85818FBB34CF695503470B623EB31.ashx (accessed March 2, 2012).

Jackson, Brooks. *Blacks and the Democractic Party.* April 2008. http://www.factcheck.org/2008/04/blacks-and-the-democratic-party/ (accessed March 1, 2012).

Jefferson, Thomas. "Full text of "The Writings of Thomas Jefferson"." September 1899. http://www.archive.org/stream/writingsofthomas10jeffiala/writingsofthomas10jeffiala_djvu.txt (accessed February 28, 2012).

—. "Notes on the State of Virginia." *Yale Law School.* 1781. http://avalon.law.yale.edu/18th_century/jeffvir.asp (accessed 2012).

—. *Thomas Jefferson Notes on the State of Virginia.* Online ebook Edition. 1782.

Jeffress, Robert, interview by Lawrence O'Donnell. "Campaigning for Christ." *The Last Word with Lawrence O'Donnell.* MSNBC. 2012.

Jilani, Zaid. *Tea Party Nation President Says It 'Makes a Lot of Sense' to Restrict Voting Only to Property Owners.* November 30, 2010. http://thinkprogress.org/politics/2010/11/30/132532/tea-party-voting-property/?mobile=nc (accessed March 2, 2012).

Katchen, Drew. *Graham: Santorum, Gingrich Christians; You have to ask Obama if he is.* February 21, 2012. http://mojoe.msnbc.msn.com/_news/2012/02/21/10466963-graham-santorum-gingrich-christians-you-have-to-ask-obama-if-he-is (accessed March 2, 2012).

Kennedy, D, James, and Jerry Newcombe. *How Would Jesus Vote?* Colorado Springs: WaterBrook Press, 2008.

Bibliography

Kennedy, John F. "Kennedy to the Greater Houston Ministerial Association." *John F. Kennedy Presidential Library and Museum.* September 12, 1960. http://www.jfklibrary.org/Asset-Viewer/ALL6YEBJMEKYGMCntnSCvg.aspx (accessed March 2, 2012).

Killough, Ashley. *Santorum on controversial remark: I was 'tongue-tied'.* January 4, 2012. http://politicalticker.blogs.cnn.com/2012/01/04/santorum-on-controversial-remark-i-was-tongue-tied/ (accessed March 2, 2012).

King, Martin Luther Jr. "How Should a Christian View Communism?" In *20 Centuries of Great Preaching: An Encyclopedia of Preaching,* by Clyde E. Jr Fant and William M. Jr Pinson, 371-378. Waco: Word Books, 1971.

Koritansky, Peter. *Internet Encyclopedia of Philosophy.* 2007. http://www.iep.utm.edu/aqui-pol/#H3 (accessed February 27, 2012).

Krugman, Paul. *How Did Economists Get it So Wrong?* September 2, 2009. http://www.nytimes.com/2009/09/06/magazine/06Economic-t.html?pagewanted=all (accessed October 2011).

—. *The Conscience of a Liberal.* November 10, 2007. http://krugman.blogs.nytimes.com/2007/11/10/innocent-mistakes/ (accessed August 2011).

Kuhn, David. *Black Vote is for Kerry.* 2009. http://www.cbsnews.com/stories/2004/10/20/politics/main650482.shtml (accessed March 1, 2012).

Liberty University. *Liberty University.* September 14, 2011. http://www.luonline.com/index.cfm?PID=9002 (accessed November 2011).

Madison, James. "Memorial and Remonstrance Against Religious Assessments." *Religious Freedom.* 1785. http://religiousfreedom.lib.virginia.edu/sacred/madison_m&r_1785.html (accessed March 2012).

—. "The Federalist No. 51." February 6, 1788. http://www.constitution.org/fed/federa51.htm (accessed March 1, 2012).

Martin, William. *With God on Our Side: The Rise of the Religious Right in America.* New York: Broadway Books, 1996.

Mason, Jeff. *Romney opens 21-point lead in South Carolina: Reuters/Ipsos poll.* January 14, 2012. http://www.reuters.com/article/2012/01/14/us-usa-campaign-poll-idUSTRE80D0U420120114 (accessed March 2, 2012).

Massa, Mark. "A Catholic for President?: John F. Kennedy and the "Secular" Theology of the Houston Speech, 1960." *Journal of Church & State* 39, no. 2 (1997): 297-317.

Matthews, Chris. "MSNBC Transcripts 1-17-2012." *MSNBC.com.* January 17, 2012. http://www.msnbc.msn.com/id/46040614/ns/msnbc_tv-hardball_with_chris_matthews/t/hardball-chris-matthews-tuesday-january/#.T1DtPnlSnEY (accessed March 2, 2012).

—. "MSNBC Transcripts 1-18-2012." January 18, 2012. http://www.msnbc.msn.com/id/46061815/ns/msnbc_tv-hardball_with_chris_matthews/t/hardball-chris-matthews-wednesday-january/#.T1Dv03lSnEY (accessed March 2, 2012).

Memoli, Michael. *Mitch McConnell's remarks on 2012 draw White House ire.* October 27, 2010. http://articles.latimes.com/2010/oct/27/news/la-pn-obama-mcconnell-20101027 (accessed February 16, 2012).

Meyers, Jim. *Newt Wins Huge Praise for South Carolina Debate.* January 17, 2012. http://www.newsmax.com/Politics/south-

Bibliography

carolina-debate-gingrich/2012/01/17/id/424434 (accessed March 2, 2012).

Monticello. "Quotations on the Jefferson Memorial." *Monticello.org.* http://www.monticello.org/site/jefferson/quotations-jefferson-memorial (accessed April 2012).

Mumford, Lewis. *The Condition of Man.* New York: Harcourt Brace Jovanocivh, 1944, 1972, 1972.

National Taxpayers Union. *History of Federal Individual Income Bottom and Top Bracket Rates.* 2009. http://ntu.org/tax-basics/history-of-federal-individual-1.html (accessed April 4, 2012).

NBC Universal Television Distribution. *The Christ Matthews Show.* 2006. http://www.thechrismatthewsshow.com/html/transcript/index.php?selected=1&id=26 (accessed November 13, 2011).

New York Historical Society. *Collections by the New York Historical Society.* New York, 1849.

New York Times. *New York Times Politics.* January 22, 2012. http://elections.nytimes.com/2012/primaries/results/live/2012-01-21 (accessed March 2, 2012).

Newell, William. *Romans: Verse-by-Verse.* Grand Rapids: Kregel Publications, 1994.

Norquist, Grover, interview by Mara Liasson. "Conservative Advocate." *Morning Edition.* NPR. May 25, 2001.

NPR Fresh Air. *NPR.com.* 2011. http://www.npr.org/2011/05/02/135846486/how-some-made-millions-betting-against-the-market (accessed February 2012).

NPR/Kaiser/Kennedy School. "Poverty in America." *kff.org*. May 1, 2001. http://www.kff.org/kaiserpolls/loader.cfm?url=/commonspot/security/getfile.cfm&PageID=13806 (accessed March 2012).

Obama, Barack. "President Obama's Speech at the National Prayer Breakfast in Washington D.C." *Washington Post*. February 2012. http://www.washingtonpost.com/politics/national-prayer-breakfast-president-obamas-speech-transcript/2012/02/02/gIQAx7jWkQ_story_1.html (accessed March 2, 2012).

Olson, Mancur. "Dictatorship, Democracy, and Development." *American Political Science Review* 83, no. 3 (September 1993): 557-576.

Oxford. *Dictionaries*. 2012. http://oxforddictionaries.com/definition/idolatry (accessed March 2, 2012).

Pew Research Center. *A Religious Portrait of African-Americans*. January 30, 2009. http://www.pewforum.org/A-Religious-Portrait-of-African-Americans.aspx (accessed October 2011).

—. *Beyond Red vs. Blue: The Political Typology*. May 4, 2011. http://www.people-press.org/2011/05/04/beyond-red-vs-blue-the-political-typology/ (accessed October 2011).

—. *Changing Faiths: Latinos and the Transformation of American Religion*. April 25, 2007. http://www.pewhispanic.org/2007/04/25/ii-religion-and-demography/ (accessed March 28, 2012).

—. *When Labels Don't Fit: Hispanics and Their Views of Identity*. April 4, 2012. http://www.pewhispanic.org/2012/04/04/when-labels-dont-fit-hispanics-and-their-views-of-identity/ (accessed April 6, 2012).

Bibliography

Pew Research. *Growing Number of Americans Believe Obama is a Muslim.* August 19, 2010. http://pewresearch.org/pubs/1701/poll-obama-muslim-christian-church-out-of-politics-political-leaders-religious (accessed February 2012).

PolitiFact.com. "John Boehner say Bush tax cuts created 8 million jobs over 10 years." *Politifact.com.* May 2011. http://www.politifact.com/truth-o-meter/statements/2011/may/11/john-boehner/john-boehner-says-bush-tax-cuts-created-8-million-/ (accessed March 2012).

Politifact.com. *Newt Gingrich Defends calling Barack Obama "food stamp president.".* 2011. http://www.politifact.com/truth-o-meter/statements/2011/may/16/newt-gingrich/newt-gingrich-defends-calling-barack-obama-food-st/ (accessed February 28, 2012).

Republican National Committee. "MSNBC." *RNC Unity Principle.* 2010. http://msnbcmedia.msn.com/i/MSNBC/Sections/NEWS/A_Politics/Reagan_First_Read.pdf (accessed March 5, 2012).

Roach, David. *LifeWay: Biblical Solutions for Life.* 2011. http://www.lifeway.com/ArticleView?storeId=10054&catalogId=10001&langId=-1&article=Research-LifeWay-Poll-Pastors-say-Mormons-not-Christians (accessed February 12, 2012).

Rutenberg, Jim. *New York Times.* June 2, 2006. http://www.nytimes.com/2006/06/02/washington/02cnd-bush.html?_r=1&oref=slogin (accessed March 2012).

Sahadi, Jeanne. *Taxes: What people forget about Reagan.* September 12, 2010. http://money.cnn.com/2010/09/08/news/economy/reagan_years_taxes/index.htm (accessed March 2012).

Sawhill, Isabell. "Getting Ahead or Losing Ground: Economic Mobility in America." *Economic Mobility Project*. February 2008. http://www.economicmobility.org/assets/pdfs/EMP_Overview.pdf (accessed August 2011).

Shah, Dayna. "General Accounting Office." *GAO.com*. January 23, 2004. http://www.gao.gov/new.items/d04353r.pdf (accessed February 20, 2012).

With God on Our Side. Directed by Calvin Skaggs, David Van Talyor and Ali Pomeroy. Produced by Lumiere Productions, Inc. 2004.

Smith, Adam. "Book I -Chapter II: Of the Principle which gives Occasion to the Division of Labor." Chap. II in *An Inquiry into the Nature and Causes of The Wealth of Nations*. Public Domain, 1776.

Smith, Adam. "Book IV- Chapter II: Of Restraints upon the Importation from Foreign Countries of such Goods as can be Produced at Home." Chap. 4 in *An Inquiry into the Nature and Causes of the Wealth of Nations*. Public Domain, 1776.

Smith, Adam. "Of the Revenue of the Sovereign or Commonwealth." In *An Inuiry into the Nature and Causes of the Wealth of Nations*, by Adam Smith. 1776.

Smith, Efrem. *God's Kingdom Over Political Ideology*. February 24, 2011. http://www.efremsmith.com/category/blog/2011/02/gods-kingdom-over-political-ideology/ (accessed February 19, 2012).

Solon, Gary. "Intergenerational Income Mobility." *The American Economic Review*, June 1992: 393-408.

Southern Baptist Convention. "On Capital Punishment." *Southern Baptist Convention*. June 2000. http://www.sbc.net/resolutions/amResolution.asp?ID=299 (accessed February 2012).

Bibliography

Southern Poverty Law Center. *Hate Group Numbers Up by 54% Since 2000.* 2009. http://www.splcenter.org/get-informed/news/hate-group-numbers-uphttp://www.splcenter.org/get-informed/news/hate-group-numbers-up (accessed February 20, 2012).

Spurgeon, Charles H. *Sermons, Volume 6.* New York: Sheldon & Company, 1859.

Stout, David. *The New York Times.* 2004. http://www.nytimes.com/2004/02/24/politics/24CND-GAY.html?pagewanted=all (accessed March 1, 2012).

Strickland, Ruth Ann. "Abortion: Pro Choice Versus Pro-Life." In *Moral Controversies in American Politics*, by Raymond Tatalovich and Byron Daynes, 3-44. Armonk: M.E. Sharpe, 2011.

Sumner, William Graham. *What Social Classes Owe Each Other.* Caldwell: Caxton Printers, 1883, 1974.

Tentmaker.com. *Scripture References to Usury, Interest.* 2012. http://www.tentmaker.org/lists/UsuryScriptureList.html (accessed August 2012).

The Barna Group, Ltd. *New Marriage and Divorce Statistics Released.* 2008. http://www.barna.org/barna-update/article/15-familykids/42-new-marriage-and-divorce-statistics-released (accessed January 19, 2012).

The Leadership Conference. *State of Hate: White Supremacist Groups Growing.* http://www.civilrights.org/publications/hatecrimes/white-supremacist.html (accessed December 2011).

The Lockman Foundation. *Amplified Bible.* Grand Rapids: Zondervan, 1954, 1958, 1962, 1964, 1965, 1987.

Thomas Nelson, Inc. *What Does the Bible Say About...* Nashville: Thomas Nelson, Inc., 2001.

Washington, George. "Washington's Inaugural Address of 1789: A Transcription." *National Archives and Records Administration*. April 30, 1789. http://www.archives.gov/exhibits/american_originals/inaugtxt.html (accessed March 2012).

Williams, Carol. *Los Angeles Times*. February 23, 2012. http://articles.latimes.com/2012/feb/23/local/la-me-0223-doma-20120223 (accessed March 15, 2012).

Wind, Rebecca. "Guttmacher Institute Media Center." September 6, 2005. http://www.guttmacher.org/media/nr/2005/09/06/index.html (accessed August 2011).

YouTube. *Town Hall Illinois 11-14-09 We All Have to Pay*. 2009. http://www.youtube.com/watch?v=ATQgrHGMSqM (accessed September 2011).

Zinn, Maxine. "Family, Race, and Poverty in the Eighties." *Signs* 14, no. 4 (1989): 856-874.

Index

10th Amendment, see States' Rights

A

A Voter's Guide for Serious Christians, 38

Abominations, 41, 68

Abortion, x, 17, 28, 42, 43, 46, 47, 52, 138

    among Christians, 63

    how to decrease, 53, 56, 65

    preventative programs, 59

    primary reasons for, Ch 5

    US statistics, 59, 60, 65

    underlying causes, 60-62,

Absolutes, 57, 65, 85, 162-163

Abstinence, 63

Adams, John, 190

African Americans, Ch 6

    on abortion, 89

    on gay rights, 89
    religiosity, 89, 97, 101
    see also liberation theology

    voting, 89

Agnostics, xi, 192

American By Heart (Palin), 205

American Dream, 126, 149

Amoral Political Parties, x, 23

Anger, 32, 77-81

    loosing ourselves in, 82

    towards God, 162

    towards the poor, 143

Anger Politics, 84, 85, 87-89

Appearance of Normality, 73

Aquinas, Thomas, 47

Atheists, xi, 178, 184, 191-192

Atonement, 40

B

Bank Overdraft Fees, 128

Barclay, William, 138-139

Battle of Jericho, 37

Benefit from the Government, 140, 144,

Benevolence of the Butcher, 126, 133

Benevolent Father, 28-29

Berwick, Donald, 79

Biblical Endorsement of,

    Capitalism, 115, 120

    Communism, 120

    Slavery, 120

    Socialism, 120

Biblical Freedom, see Oppressive Freedom

Biblical Influence in America, Ch 3

Biblical Interpretation, Ch 8

Biblical Morality, Int, Ch 8

Biblical Right to Choose, Ch 5

Biblical Story of

    "Render unto Caesar", 80, 138

    Daniel, 199-201

    Joseph, 17, 199-201

    Joshua, 37-38

    Prodigal Son, 26, 29, 32-33

    Three Hebrew Boys, 200-201

Big Brother, 28

Big Government, 99

Billings, Robert, 20

Black Liberation Theology, 96-99
Black Religious Conservatives, 89, 93, 96, 97, 101

Black Republicans, 90, 95

Blackwell, Morton, 20

Blitzer, Wolf, 77

Book of
- Deuteronomy, 117, 118
- Exodus, 117
- Ezekiel, 117
- First John, 77
- Galatians, 197
- Isaiah, 40, 109, 112, 113, 170
- Joshua, 37, 38, 48
- Leviticus, 68, 116
- Luke, 25, 172
- Mark, 144
- Matthew, 41, 80, 83, 137, 138, 140, 144, 159, 171, 179, 196
- Proverbs, 68, 69
- Romans, 79, 138, 178, 182, 184, 187,
- Third John, 78
- Timothy, 44, 125

Brookhaven, Mississippi, 204

Brookings Institution, 148
Brown v the Board of Education, 99

Bush Tax Cuts, 141, 142, 145

Bush, George H.W., 43

Bush, George W., 19, 43, 58, 141

C

Cain, Herman, 90, 95

Calvinism, *notes 214*

Capitalism, unregulated, 128

Carlson, Tucker, 45

Carnegie, Andrew, 130

Carter, Jimmy, 16, 17, 21
Catholic Church, 100, 107, 108, 172, 177

Catholic President, 177

Centers for Medicare & Medicaid, 79

Character of a Christian, 196-198
Charity, 28, 39, 83, 84, 87, 104, 110, 118-120, 163-166

Cheering for Death, 78

Children of Israel, 96
Christ like, see Character of a Christian

Christ the Liberator, 96

Christian duty to the Poor, 83
Christianity, requirements of salvation, 178
Christianity, true role in politics, 195, 201
Christianity, true, see Character of a Christian

Christ's constituency, 159

Churchill, Winston, 149

Civil Rights Act of 1964, 90, 99
Civil Rights Movement, 90, 96, 98, 99
Civil Unions, see Marriage Equality

Class Warfare, 162

Classical economic theory, 104

Clausewitz, Carl Von, 169

Clinton, Bill, 43, 71

CNN, 77

Cognitive Dissonance, 57, 208

Cold War, 115

Colson, Charles, 19
Communism, 109, 115, 116, 120, 149,

Conception, 59

Confession of faith, 178, 179

Conservatism, 160, 167
Conservative Religion, 157, 160, 162, 163, 165-167
Constitution, 10, 11, 27, 29, 30, 44, 70, 75, 131, 140

Index

Contradictions, 57, 169, 170-172

Coral Ridge Presbyterian, 37, 206

Corporate Welfare, 81, 111, 141, 146

Coulter, Ann, 163

Crucifixion of Christ, 40, 195

D

Death Penalty, 39, 167, 172

Death Row, 172

Debate Audiences, *see* Republican Debate Audiences

Defense of Marriage Act, 71

Democratic Party, 9, 22, 58, 59, 62, 89, 90, 100, 101, 169

Diamond, Sara, *notes* 211-214

Divorce Rates in Church, 64

Dixiecrats, 90

Don't Ask Don't Tell, 73

Dr. Martin Luther King Day, 93

Dream Act, *notes* 216, 222

E

Economic Collapse, *see* Great Recession

Economic Growth, 32, 104, 130, 140, 142

Economic Inequality, 28, 107-111, 124, 148, 149

Economic Mobility, 148, 149, 153

Economic Oppression, 97, 102

Economic Policy, 105, 161

Economic Recovery Tax Act of 1981, 141

Effects of conservatism on Christianity, *see* Conservative Religion

Eisegetical Interpretations, 120, 180

Emergency Room Care, 84

Emergency Room Costs, 84, 208

Enron, 127

Euthanasia, 38

Evangelical Coalition,

    Disrespect for, 45
    Symbiotic relationship, 157-160

F

Faith, "I told you so" faith, 198

False Dichotomy, 49, 55

False Religion, 160

Falwell, Jerry, 15, 20, 42, 45, 48, 157, 158

Falwell, Jerry, Jr., 158,

First Amendment, *see* Religious Freedoms

Flat Tax, 143, 144

Florida Atlantic University, 51

Food Stamps, 91, 92

Food Stamps President, 92

Forced Morality, 34

Form of Godliness, 44, 160

Fort Lauderdale, Florida, 37, 206

Founding Fathers, 187, 191

Fox News, 93

Franklin, Benjamin, 132, 191

Free Market Utopianism, 129-131

Free Market, 123, 128-131, 150, *See also* Capitalism

Free Will, 29, 30, 46, 47

Free Will, God grants, 29

Fruits of the Spirit, 198

Fukuyama, Francis, 149

G

Gay Rights, 67

    Opposition of, 10, 38, 73,
    Republican Manipulation of, 67

General Accounting Office, 71

Gilded Age, 130

Gingrich, Newt, 92-95, 179

God's Political Ideology, 37-38, 206

Goldwater, Barry, 45

GOProud, 67

Government intervention, 29, 110, 129, 130

Grace, extending, 172

Graham, Billy, 19, 115, 179

Graham, Franklin, 179

Great Recession, 148

Greed, 97, 126, 128

Gun Control, 158

Guttmacher Institute, see Abortion Statistics

H

Harris-Perry, Melissa, 96, 98, 99

Healthcare, 28, 62, Chapter 5

Heaven, Republican Heaven, Ch 11

Holiness, our duty in obtaining, 47-48

Homosexuality, 17, 39, 41, 42, 43, 47, 68, 69,72-75,

How Would Jesus Vote? (Kennedy), 37, 232

Human Secularists, 184, 192

I

Idols, 183,
    see also Conservative Religion

If I be lifted up, 195

Income Taxes, 143, 144

Individual Freedom, 28, 31-33

Insurance, *see* Healthcare

Interest, 117, 118, See also Usury

Invisible Hand, 126, 129, 188 See also Adam Smith

Iowa Primaries, 43

It Takes Money to Make Money, 152

J

Jefferson, Thomas, 107, 112, 189

Jefress, Robert Dr., 183

Jesus Christ, Ch 2
    character and essence, *see* Character of a Christian

    drawing ability, 96

    Hatred of, 167, 196

Jim Crow, 96, 204

Job Creators, 111, 126, 152

Johnson, Lyndon, 90-91

Jones, William, 96

Justice, *see* Social Justice

K

Kant, Immanuel, 127

Kennedy, Dr. D. James, 15, 37, 48, 20

Kennedy, John F., 177

Kids for Cash, 127

King, Martin Luther, Jr., 93, 120

Kingdom of God, 115, 120, 121, 201, 205

L

Legislating Morality, *See also* Oppressive Freedom and Free Will

LGBT, Lesbian Gay Bisexual and Transgendered, *See Gay Rights*

Liberation Theology, *See Black Liberation Theology*

Liberty University, Ch 11

Liberty, Ch 3, Ch 5

Limited Role of Government, 28

Lincoln, Abraham, 90

Love of Money, 125

Low Waged Labor, 109, 110

Index

M

Madison, James, 129, 188

Majority Consensus, 31

Marriage, Biblical definition, 67, 70, 71, 75

Marriage, Government's role, 70

Marriage Equality, 67, 68, 71, 72, 75

Marriage, traditional definition, Ch 7

Marriage, Traditional, 67

Martin, William, *notes* 211-214, 222

Marxism, 120

Matthews, Chris, 45, 95

McAteer, Ed, 20

McConnell, Mitch, 82

Meet the Press, 16

Mega Churches, 98, 182

Middle Class, 104, 141, 142, 143, 145, 148, 151, 153

Midterm Elections of 2010, 84

Ministry Mailing Lists, 18, 20

Miraculous Healing, 79

Moral Majority, 20, 21, 141

Moral Quality of an Action, *see* Immanuel Kant

Mormonism, 182

Mother's Testimony Booed, 88

Mumford, Lewis, 115, 116,

N

NAACP, 92

National Affairs Briefing, 15, 17

National Maturity, 32

Nebuchadnezzar, 201

New Jersey's 6th Congressional District, 87

Newell, William, 185

Nixon Administration, 19

Nixon, Richard, 19, 91

Non-Christian Presidents, 184

Norquist, Grover, *notes* 227, 235

O

Obama, Barack, 53-55,58, 61, 92,

   Faith of, 178, 181, 183

   Father of, 178

   Opposition of, 82, 183

   Prayer Breakfast, 179

Obama, Malia and Sasha, 53

Obamacare, 77, 81, 82, 88, *See also Patient Protection and Affordable Care Act*

O'Conner, Sandra Day, 42, 45

Ohio Protest, 87

Old South, 91

Olson, Mancur, 139

Oppression, 41, 96, 97, 102, 112, 116, 167

Oppressive Freedom, Ch 3, *See also Free Will*

Outcomes vs Opportunity, 149-150

Outsourcing, 125

Oval Office, 19

P

Palin, Sarah, 205

Palm Beach County Florida, 207

Parkinson's Protestor, 87

Party of Christ, 78, 204

Patient Protection and Affordable Care Act, 77, see also Obamacare

Paul, Ron, 77

Pauper, 130, 143, *See also Poverty*

Perceptions of God, 99,

245

see also Black Liberation Theology

Perry, Rick, 158, 167

Pew Research, 148-150

Phillips, Howard, 20

Phony Theology, 179-180

Political Manipulation, 10, 11, 61, 191

Political Parties, Ch 1
Political Power, 22, 44, 46, 49, 85, 131, 165, 200
Political Radicalism, see Radicalism,

Political Rhetoric, 61, 74

Pompano Beach, Florida, 206

Pontius Pilate, 185
Poverty, 28, 39, 64, 65, 97, 109-110, 188, 119, 124, 133, 134, 145, 148, 150, 153
Prayer in School, 17, 42, 140, 192, 198

Preexisting Conditions, 87
Presidential Election of 1976, 16-18, 21
Presidential Election of 1980, 15-17, 21, 42, 44, 140

Presidential Election of 1988, 43
Presidential Election of 2000, 43, 141
Presidential Election of 2012, see Republican Primaries of 2012

Prince of Peace, 169-170
Private Charity, 39, 84, 110, 118, 119
Pro Choice, 51, 55, 56, 58, 59, 61-65, 181
Pro Life Demonstration, 51, 53, 54, 58, 60, 61
Pro-Life Movement, 53, 56, 58-61, 64, 65
Pro Life, Pro Choice Alliance, 64-65
Progressive Taxation, 145, 150, 151

Prosperity Gospel, 97-99

Protestantism, 115

Public Housing, 91

R

Race Baiting, 91, 95

Racism, 91, 93-97, 101

Radical Islamists, 41

Radicalism, 165
Reagan, Ronald, 16-18, 22, 42, 91, 140, 157, 161, 203

Reagan's Unity Principle, 161
Redistribution of Wealth, 79, 81, 104, 118

Rehnquist, William, 58

Religious Absolutes, *See Absolutes*
Religious freedom, 31, 46, 70, 74, 184

Religious tests for office, 177
Render unto Caesar, see Biblical Story of Caesar
Reproductive Rights, 28, see also Abortions
Republican Party Tax Policies, 141, 142
Republican Debate Audiences, 78, 167
Republican Party Economic Policies, 97, 104, 105, 111, 166
Republican Party Platform, 67, 97, 111,

Republican Presidential Debate, 77

Republican Primaries of 2012, 91

Resolving Tension, 57, 204

Robertson, Pat, 22, 43, 48

Robison, James, 15, 16, 22, 48

Rockefeller, John D., 130

Roe v. Wade, 17, 43, 58, 59, 64

Romans 10:9, 178, 182, 187

Romney, Mitt, 182

S

Index

Santorum, Rick, 92, 179

Sawhill, Isabel, 148

Segregation, 94, 96, 99

Self Righteousness, 9, 68, 165

Self Sabotage of the Pro Life Movement, 53

Sermon on the Mount, 171

Sexual Morality, 39, 48, 63

Sexual Morality, in the Church, 63

Shari 'a Law, 41

Sheep/Shepherd, 22

Sin, measuring of, 40

Smith, Adam, see *Wealth of Nations*

Smith, Efrem, 120

Social Darwinism, 130

Social Justice, 39, 99-101, 107-112, 128

Social Mobility, 149

Social Morality, 41, 97, 104, 112, 146, 153

Social Security and FICA Taxes, 143

Social Welfare, 111, 141, 146

Socialism, 79, 108, 109, 112, 120, 149

Societal norms, 73-74

South Carolina Debates, 93

South Carolina Primaries, 93-95

Southern Baptist Convention, 172

Southern Democrats, see Dixiecrats

Southern Strategy, 91-93

Southern Vote, 91

Space Shuttle Challenger, 203

Spurgeon, Charles, 138, 181

States' Rights Advocates, 99

States' Rights, 91, 99

Stem-cell Research, 38

Sumner, William Graham, 130, 131

Supply Side Theory, *See Trickle-Down Economics*

Supreme court, 42, 43, 45, 46, 58, 59

T

Tampa, Florida, 77

Tax Burden, 140-145, 152

Tax Subsidies, 81

Taxation, 138-140

Tea Party, 85, 160

Televangelists, 18, 159, 206

Texas, 158, 182

The Condition of Man, (Mumford) 115, 116

The End of History and the Last Man, (Fukuyama) 149, 230

Tickle-Down Economics, 140, 142, 153, 161,

Truman, Harry, 19

Tulane University, 96

U

United States Credit Rating, 158

Unrestrained Freedom, *See Oppressive Freedom*

Usury, 117

V

Vanderbilt, Cornelius, 130

Viguerie, Richard, 20

W

Wages of Sin, 172

War, 39, 40, 140, 149, 169, 170

Washington, George, 188

Wealth Disparity, 148, 162

Wealth of Nations, The, (Smith), 126-132, 150, 151

Welfare Queens, 91

West, Allen, 95

Weyrich, Paul, 20

What God hates, *See Abominations*

White Extremism, 91
White House, 19, 42, 43, 58, 179, 185

White, Byron, 58

Widow's Mite, 144

Williams, Juan, 93-94
Women's Rights, 28, 53, 55, 56, 65

Working Poverty, 109

X

Xenophobia, 161

Y

Year of the Evangelical, 18

Young Bucks, 91

Made in the USA
Lexington, KY
04 June 2015